Praise for *Trust*

"*Trust* deals with entrepreneurs across the developing world, where creativity is sorely needed. Khanna weaves together stories of conventional and social enterprises in the private sector and in government. He recognizes the enormous promise of technology—but to be used wisely. A highly readable and must-read narrative!"
—**Nandan Nilekani, cofounder of Infosys Technologies and Founding Chairman, Unique Identification Authority of India (Aadhaar)**

"Trust is central to any enterprise, and this is especially true across countries in Latin America and the developing world, as Khanna suggests it must be. We work hard to build and maintain it with our customers, employees, bankers, suppliers, investors, and public authorities. Trust is by far more important than simply counting on the rule of law or our institutions. It is the vital underpinning of our growth and prosperity through thick and thin."
—**Woods Staton, Chairman, Arco Dorado, Mexico**

"Khanna studies the core of the matter for entrepreneurship in emerging markets. Entrepreneurs in such markets face a 'friction-full' environment. As a friend of mine says, 'We live in a market economy with Soviet scaffolding' and because of this everything needs to be negotiated—nothing happens by itself. And why does this happen? The answer is lack of trust!"
—**Álvaro Rodríguez Arregui, cofounder and Managing Partner, IGNIA, Mexico**

"Khanna's book is right on target in spotlighting the supreme importance of trust not just in private entrepreneurship but in all connections between entrepreneurs and government, civil society, and people. As Khanna's examples compellingly demonstrate, building and maintaining healthy levels of trust is crucial for human progress."
—**Muhammad Ali Pate, former Minister of State for Health, Nigeria**

"Khanna skillfully and convincingly argues that trust is a core part of the enabling environment that civil society and the state must foster to enable enterprising individuals to help themselves. I would recommend it to all interested in private sector development."
—**Emmanuel Jimenez, Executive Director, International Initiative for Impact Evaluation (3ie), India**

"Challenges abound across the developing world, and it's up to us to address them and not wait for the government or for charity. My experiences as an entrepreneur across Africa make me appreciate Khanna's focus on weaving a web of trust to get everyone focused, very practically, on how ventures get built and how they scale across large populations. I hope young people everywhere are inspired by this book's 'can-do' spirit."

—**Mo Ibrahim, founder of Celtel International and founder and Chair, Mo Ibrahim Foundation, Africa**

TRUST

Other books by Tarun Khanna

Winning in Emerging Markets:
A Road Map for Strategy and Execution

Billions of Entrepreneurs: How China and India
Are Reshaping Their Futures—and Yours

TRUST

Creating the Foundation for
Entrepreneurship in Developing Countries

TARUN KHANNA

BK

Berrett–Koehler Publishers, Inc.
a BK Business book

Berrett-Koehler Publishers, Inc.
1333 Broadway, Suite 1000
Oakland, CA 94612-1921
Tel: (510) 817-2277
Fax: (510) 817-2278
www.bkconnection.com

ORDERING INFORMATION

Quantity sales. Special discounts are available on quantity purchases by corporations, associations, and others. For details, contact the "Special Sales Department" at the Berrett-Koehler address above. Individual sales. Berrett-Koehler publications are available through most bookstores. They can also be ordered directly from Berrett-Koehler: Tel: (800) 929-2929; Fax: (802) 864-7626; www.bkconnection.com. Orders for college textbook course adoption use. Please contact Berrett-Koehler: Tel: (800) 929-2929; Fax: (802) 864-7626.

Distributed to the U.S. trade and internationally by Penguin Random House Publisher Services.

Berrett-Koehler and the BK logo are registered trademarks of Berrett-Koehler Publishers, Inc.

Printed in the United States of America.

Berrett-Koehler books are printed on long-lasting acid-free paper. When it is available, we choose paper that has been manufactured by environmentally responsible processes. These may include using trees grown in sustainable forests, incorporating recycled paper, minimizing chlorine in bleaching, or recycling the energy produced at the paper mill.

Library of Congress Cataloging-in-Publication Data

Names: Khanna, Tarun, author.
Title: Trust : creating foundations for entrepreneurship in developing countries / Tarun Khanna.
Description: Oakland, California : Berrett-Koehler Publishers, [2018] | Includes bibliographical references.
Identifiers: LCCN 2018008179 | ISBN 9781523094837 (pbk.)
Subjects: LCSH: Social responsibility of business--Developing countries. | Trust--Developing countries. | Entrepreneurship--Developing countries. | Consumers--Developing countries. | Customer relations--Developing countries.
Classification: LCC HD60.5.D44 K43 2018 | DDC 338/.04091724--dc23
LC record available at https://lccn.loc.gov/2018008179

First Edition
25 24 23 22 21 20 19 18   10 9 8 7 6 5 4 3 2 1

Book producer and text designer: Steven Hiatt/Hiatt & Dragon, San Francisco
Copyeditor: Mark Woodworth   Proofreader: Tom Hassett   Cover designer: Mayapriya Long
Illustrations: Mahima Kachroo   Indexer: Theresa Duran

To Mom and Dad

Contents

Preface

I have been studying entrepreneurs in developing countries for about two decades. Initially my work was with incumbent enterprises, often in the form of large family-run businesses. Along the way, though, it was curious to see how the new kids on the block nonetheless forced their way into contention, despite having the deck stacked against them. Established companies had much readier access to scarce money and talent, and they knew how to deal with often-corrupt corridors of power. But that did not stop new entrepreneurs from finding chinks in the armor of the old guard.

Then, less than a decade ago, I began supporting young entrepreneurs as an angel investor, and soon after, I started my own enterprises in the developing world. I connect and advise the surplus talent and a flood of ideas in Cambridge, where I work, with the huge opportunities and need for insight in the developing world.

I have found this work to be intensely creative . . . and exhilarating! In fact, I find entrepreneurship-in-the-field and my academic work to be entirely symbiotic, if perhaps unusual (or so I'm told).

In this short book, comprising a few illustrative stories, I've tried to distill some of the patterns I've found. None of the stories here are about my own ventures, though the accounts are informed by them. Rather, these are individual entrepreneurs and settings I've studied and worked with in myriad capacities, usually each in multiple ways and for a few years, and sometimes for more than a decade.

The themes in the chapters also directly inform my own entrepreneurial efforts. For example, coming face-to-face with the visceral distrust that consumers routinely display when looking for all manner of daily consumables—suspecting vendors of either being incompetent or unscrupulous—led me to co-found Aspiring Minds, a machine-learning talent assessment firm that uses technology to certify the quality of talent all over Asia, operating from its offices in Beijing, New Delhi, and Manila. Aspiring Minds helps cement trust in the ecosystem by connecting youth to economic opportunities.

Similarly, my encounters with technology—whether in connecting small vendors to global commerce in China or the use of advanced biometrics in India—has alerted me to its incredible promise, but also to the usually overlooked need to situate the technology in its specific problem-centered milieu. This is a lesson I've taken to heart in a tea chain that's located across India, Chaipoint. We have started using robots, developed in Shenzhen, to make quality tea at large scale in the Asian way—so-called *chai*. We have learned to do this in a way that respects centuries-old rituals of tea drinking.

Throughout all this, a central facet of this book, and of my work over past decades, is to recognize that problems cannot be easily modularized and tackled in bits and pieces in the developing world. Getting capital to a capital-starved person isn't much use if her health is compromised or she has no means to travel somewhere to use it. A change of mindset is needed to move away from the idea that entrepreneurs should be laser-focused on the problems they want to solve—as they do in locales like Boston and San Francisco—to a mindset that emphasizes that they don't have that luxury in the developing world. They must do that, and more—they must *create the conditions to create*. The book's stories of the heart-surgeon entrepreneur from Bangalore and the unlikely multinational social entrepreneur from Bangladesh provide sharp illustrations of this mindset change.

This reasoning applies equally to so-called for-profit entrepreneurs and those motivated more by a desire to achieve social progress. I've also encountered a hearteningly large number of entrepreneurs working within the state in country after country—in this book, I discuss such efforts in Brazil and India. Normally, we think of bureaucracy and entrepreneurship as oxymoronic. My experiences suggest that this need not be so, something I commented on in a prior book narrating earlier experiences in China and India, *Billions of Entrepreneurs* (Harvard Business Press; Penguin in South Asia, 2008). So I hew to a rather broad view of entrepreneurship rather than one focused only on hotshots taking companies public.

I'd be thrilled if this book led entrepreneurs—and those interested in entrepreneurship as the key to economic advance—to reflect on their experiences, and perhaps coaxed some would-be entrepreneurs to jump into the fray!

I'm grateful to all the entrepreneurs I've had an opportunity to work with, those in the book and numerous others, for teaching me so much. Similarly, the luxury of being at an institution like Harvard, a crossroads for talented students, is difficult to overemphasize. Numerous research assistants have helped over the years, especially those spread at Harvard's centers across the developing world, several linked to Harvard Business School and the university's Lakshmi Mettal South Asia Institute, which I currently have the privilege of leading. Most directly, though, I am thankful to Jonathan Mingle, who worked with me on the manuscript a couple of years ago, to Carolyn Brown this past year for a herculean effort to help it across the finish line, and to Mahima Kachroo, who helped with the lovely pencil illustrations.

On a daily basis, I owe my wife, Ruhi, and teenage daughter and son, Simran and Rishi, much affection and a massive debt of gratitude for support that's too extensive to describe in detail. My daughter and my sister, Latika, kindly read early parts of the text. But it's time to dedicate this work specifically to my mom and dad, who've remained my role models throughout my adult life. I do this with heartfelt thanks and no small measure of pride in them.

Tarun Khanna
Boston, February 2018

Introduction

Trust, Entrepreneurship, and the Developing World

Entrepreneurs with great ideas to address problems and opportunities in developing countries cannot rely on the usual foundations—laws, regulatory oversight, and government protections—as they might in the developed world, because such foundations are incipient or don't even exist. Good ideas from such countries can easily morph into failed ones—coupled with acrimony and mistrust—if an entrepreneur inadvertently presumes on the sustenance of phantom, trust-enhancing societal foundations. Rather, the entrepreneurial solution is to embrace the situation and to explicitly focus on nurturing trust as a complement to the problem being solved, in myriad ways that I will explore in this book. The entrepreneur must not just create, but must also create the conditions to create.

Ambient Trust

This may seem prosaic and pedestrian, but think for a minute about how we get things done in many parts of the United States. When you have an urge to buy something, the web seamlessly and instantly provides the information you need; when your faucet

1

leaks, several plumbers, all rated by reliability, are at hand to fix it. If the plumber you hire doesn't do a good job, there are ways to take him to task. A decade ago, my then five-year-old son locked himself in a basement room. We called the Newton city police. They were at our doorstep to unlock the door in less than ten minutes. Now, Newton—an affluent, well-run suburb of Boston—might be different from other parts of the United States. Still, in our part of the world, the conditions generally exist to summon whatever we need to just get on with life.

It's more than that, too. If a courier service leaves large packages on my doorstep, I trust that someone won't grab them and run. I often leave my garage door open at home, or my office door at work. I'm not trying to tempt fate, simply responding naturally to the empirical reality that, other than having suffered a minor burglary in New York City once, three decades of safety have bred in me this trust in urban life in East Coast USA. Arrangements that permeate daily life engender that kind of trust in much of the developed world.

Indeed, if you think about it, without this ambient trust, the workings of just about *everything* would be compromised. If I hesitated to call the local police when my son accidentally locked himself in the basement—perhaps because I thought they wouldn't respond or I feared I'd be shaken down for a side-payment (*baksheesh*)—no amount of their discipline and training would be of much use.

As an angel investor, I often hand off money to a would-be entrepreneur. I trust her to use it for the purposes intended. It's true that if some ethical lapse or fraud occurs, I can resort to accountants and lawyers and regulators to seek redress. But these are likelier to be institutions of last resort after informal means have failed—say, efforts to preserve her reputation, or the threat of blackballing her from future endeavors. Further, the use of the formal entities would require me to trust *them* in the first instance.

. . .

This role of trust applies to more complex endeavors as well. Near my office is Harvard's Wyss Institute for Biologically Inspired Engineering (called "Wyss" for short). Some years ago, I got to know a scientist there who came from Dublin named Conor Walsh, who founded the Harvard Biodesign Lab to help create wearable robotic devices. These have a range of uses, from rehabilitating accident victims to enabling soldiers to lug heavy materiel in combat. The lab itself is a perpetual beehive of activity, with prototypes of prosthetics that range from the bizarre to uncannily natural-looking, sensors strewn around, the background hum of pneumatic actuators and the more grating sounds of specialized saws, even tailors working with customized fabric to clothe the robotic devices.

The Wyss scientists must often work collectively with the patients whose needs they are trying to address. This requires the patients to be ferried to the labs where they can be fitted with, say, a robotic sleeve that lets someone paralyzed from the waist down partly stand, so that his limited mobility can be measured with sensors and devices. If you think about it, there is a range of different types of expertise that Walsh's team needs to access to get this right. They need to understand the anatomic particulars of each patient to get the material and fitting correct, they have to understand the incredibly complex field of medical pain management, and they probably must get a handle on patient psychology as well. Conor Walsh is a smart guy, yet these aren't his sweet spots. He has to tap into the goodwill and collaboration of folks from different backgrounds so that he can do his thing. Here at the Wyss, then, lies a complicated web of trust.

Fortunately, the amazing thing about Cambridge is that all of these expertise pools are a literal stone's throw away. But accessing them requires that Walsh and his team be seen as worthy collaborators. Other experts trust that he and his team members will not misappropriate their input or waste their time. These specialists are perhaps confident that the expertise sharing will be reciprocated at some point. Even in the hypercompetitive world of cutting-edge research, there are rules, norms, and arrangements that protect scientists. The consequences of violating this unspoken trust are unspeakably severe. Social ostracism would surely result. Indeed, an outcast has no hope of going on to participate in the free flow of ideas that is the lifeblood of any system of science.

Conor's web of trust has to spread even further. The doctors and the medical establishment responsible for patients' well-being have to begin to trust that the biodesign folks at the Wyss Institute will work sensitively with their patients, using a skill set that engineers or tailors have not normally cultivated as part of their professional experience. All these consummate professionals must work on protocols and mutual information sharing that both cultivate and nurture this trust. Nothing gets done without it.

Then out in the world can be found literally dozens of providers of risk capital who will entertain a plausible experiment to translate Conor's research into reality. Here again, the provision of early-stage financing entails considerable trust. The scientist must trust the financier to whom he reveals his ideas in a bid for funding. What protects the scientist? The financier signs a nondisclosure agreement, of course, promising to keep the proprietary content secret. Still, the financier's desire to maintain a trustworthy reputation to ensure future dealings with such scientists is equally important.

As is suggested by these simple examples—local ones to me— trust comes in many forms. It might emanate from reputations that have been carefully cultivated over years, even decades, by frequent quotidian interactions. Trust might be initiated by referrals—that is, I work with somebody because he's referred to me by someone I trust. It's often underpinned by formal structures, laws, and regulations—public law-and-order rules, contractual practices in individual and organizational undertakings, the norms of American academia, and so on.

Always, trust oxygenates. It enlivens our existence and facilitates every interaction, whether complex or mundane, business or personal.

. . .

This idea is far from new. It goes back, in fact, to the very roots of economics itself. Adam Smith, the father of economics, may be best known for the concept of "the invisible hand," in which people following their own self-interests guide the markets to stability.[1] Indeed, Smith was right to marvel at the almost magical cumulative effect of each individual acting in her own self-interest. But even Smith emphasized the importance of trust for the functioning of markets. For him, trust was the hidden engine of economic progress.

As Smith argues in his 1759 book *Theory of Moral Sentiments,* "Frankness and openness conciliate confidence. We trust the man who seems willing to trust us. We see clearly, we think, the road by which he means to conduct us, and we abandon ourselves with pleasure to his guidance and direction. Reserve and concealment, on the contrary, call forth diffidence."[2] Smith gives some examples of the value of trust in his famed 1776 book *The Wealth of Nations,* as well: "The wages of goldsmiths and jewelers are everywhere superior to those of many other workmen, not only of equal, but of much superior ingenuity on account of the precious materials with which they are entrusted. We trust our health to the physician, our fortune, and sometimes our life and reputation, to the lawyer and attorney."[3]

Legions of academics have studied trust.* I've been extensively educated by this scholarship, of course. In this book, though, I wish to focus on a relatively underemphasized part: the idea that the creation of trust is an act both of creativity and of individual agency. Indeed, I aver that it's the closest thing to a general admonition for creating ventures that can productively shape developing societies *at scale*—that is, in more than just piecemeal ways.

. . .

Maintaining trust requires vigilance, something we've largely failed to practice in the developed world of late. Especially in the years since the global economic crisis triggered by the meltdown of the U.S. financial system in 2008—the worst since the Great Depression in the 1930s[4]—trust in business has remained low. It's not as low as trust in the media or in government, but that should offer scant comfort.[5] In this environment, entrepreneurs are suspect. It's extraordinary that it has come to this: that business, the very institution responsible for so many of the creature comforts that are becoming daily conveniences throughout the developed world—such as by leveraging the so-called gig economy to carry out simple tasks or accessing healthcare through remote video technology—is reviled by the person on the street. As one possible countermeasure, at the Harvard Business School, my colleagues began to teach corporate accountability as a mandatory course in which students are exposed to ethical dilemmas in business as a way of sensitizing them to their future responsibilities. Several of us educators laud this initiative but also maintain a healthy

* For example, economists like Douglas North, biologists like E. O. Wilson, and political scientists like Francis Fukuyama have written extensively about trust.

skepticism as to whether it's more effective than a Band-Aid on a gushing wound. Regaining a former level of trust will be necessary in the future.

What's important to note is that our trust-induced institutional arrangements do two things: They dramatically simplify daily life, and they enable collaboration to invent anew. They move societies forward. Indeed, trying to determine which comes first, trust or trust-building institutions, is a futile endeavor. They go hand in hand. The institutions can build trust over time. Yet, the institutions require that trust in their abilities be taken seriously, as well. Here, developing trust, and building institutions that create that trust, need to be part of the same conversation for virtually all entrepreneurs throughout the developing world.

Vacuums in the Developing World

Growing up in India, even in affluent areas, my family and I always had wrought iron grills on every window of our home. These were meant to keep the bad guys out, for security. They allowed us to keep the windows open, but prevented someone from clambering in off street level, or even scaling the wall of a not-too-elevated apartment complex.

We also had domestic help as far back as I can recall. Occasionally, the help had been in the family for decades, creating a paternalistic and full-trust relationship between our family and that of the help. But, on other occasions, the relationship was a short and transactional one with someone far less advantaged than us. Wariness ensued all around. We'd worry about petty theft, for example. There was no way we would leave the house unattended for a cleaning service, as we do today in Newton.

As an adult, I saw this same lack of trust elsewhere in the developing world. I have traveled frequently to Johannesburg over the last two decades, just as South Africa entered its post-apart-heid era. I commuted between the campus at Wits (University of Witwatersrand) to accommodations closer to what is now the tony enclave of Sandton and close to sprawling townships such as Alexandra.

My pleasant memories of visits with friends are marred by the recollection of security concerns. The idea that you should not keep your windows open when your car stops at a traffic light for fear of being held up at gunpoint. The fact that by entering an affluent house, you felt like you were entering a secured military encampment. Barbed wire often crowned the walls surrounding the abode. Access to friends' driveways was through underground tunnels into which you entered only with security-code authen-tication. All this was to keep out unemployed individuals whose lives were in disarray, either those from Johannesburg's townships or migrants from neighboring Zimbabwe, a country in economic free fall. This was a situation considerably worse than what my family had experienced in just "normally" untrusting India. Think about how scary it can be in such circumstances even to go to the corner convenience store—so-called *spaza* shops are heavily secured—or consider what happens when you can't even set up a corner store for fear of future violence.

Sarah Lockwood is a researcher of Zimbabwean origin at Harvard. She cofounded Mawazo—meaning "ideas" in Swahi-li, a language spoken across large swaths of Africa—which is an organization that supports small-scale social entrepreneurs in var-ious regions in Africa. She describes her personal situation this way: "Security is a huge issue here. In my neighborhood in Cape Town, for example, a middle-class suburb close to the University of Cape Town, we not only have the usual personal security for our house (high walls, automatic gates, and a complex alarm sys-tem with cameras and sensors on windows and doors), but there are also guardhouses throughout the neighborhood, manned 24/7 by private security guards who conduct regular foot, bicycle, and car patrols."[6]

This lack of trust, typical throughout South Africa, is more than simply a challenge for the people living there, however; it is part of the business landscape itself. In fact, residential, commercial, and industrial security is an industry worth billions of rand in its own right in South Africa. The number of security officers employed across the country is more than twice the number of the South African police officers. The problems with mistrust run so deep in that society that an industry watchdog is required to help establish whom to even trust to supply these security services. As the famous Roman poet Juvenal said in his work *Satires*, "*Quis custodiet ipsos custodes*"—literally, "Who will guard the guardians?"[7]

Creating trust can give a business a competitive edge in South Africa. The golf estate Dainfern cites its security expertise as a major selling point of membership. This expertise is no joke. Measures include seismic sensors in the walls and steel bars that extend 10 feet into the ground to deter potential intruders from tunneling below. Sarah describes the golf course further: "Detectors along the length of the perimeter wall listen for incursions. An electric fence tops the wall. Closed-circuit cameras. Gatehouse control-room. Rapid reaction vehicles. Frequent armed patrols. . . . All of this so residents can stroll through the neighborhood, leave their windows open at night, and their children can walk safely to the on-site school."

Even an ordinary trip to KFC in Soweto, a township of Johannesburg famous for uprisings against apartheid and now a tourist destination, requires extreme security measures. Sarah describes some of them: "At the KFC in Soweto, the counter where you order is completely barricaded by metal bars and bullet-proof glass, with just a few small gaps for you to put your money in and get your food out." The entire system there is weighed down by an extreme lack of trust.

Such distrust imposes a tremendous cognitive burden, like sand in society's wheels, which slows things down and consumes extra energy. Distrust saps one's zest for life. It has an enervating effect on attempts to be creative, to solve problems, even to just get on with daily living.

Worst of all, since we humans are all creatures of habit, we get conditioned to shrug and live with it. As Sarah elaborated regarding the KFC store, "It was only very recently that I realized that this is not normal, and not all KFCs around the world have the same level of security inside." I'd wager that quotidian realities such as these might not make the nightly news, yet they exert as big a drag on societal progress as do even some horrors of war and rampant instability in parts of the developing world.

. . .

The lack of trust worsens an already tough situation in the developing world. For example, it can be hard in those parts of the world to find simple information that's needed to get things done. Some years ago, I found myself in the hot, sultry southern Indian metropolis of Chennai looking for an ice pack to cool some medication that one of my companions needed. Fortunately, we were staying in a luxury hotel at the time. I asked the concierge to help me procure one. It turned out that such ice packs were not commonly used, so it took a while to explain what I needed, then more time for the staff to locate stores that might plausibly have these, none of which had any sort of web presence. A lot of running around ensued, and some hours later a basic ice pack emerged. I calculated that, assuming normal wage rates, about 800 rupees were spent in lost time, for something that ultimately cost Rs 20. Now, in the U.S., I'd probably spend $5 worth of time to walk over to the local pharmacy in an urban setting or drive to a semi-urban Walmart to pick it up for under $5. That is, the ratio of effort to value is 40:1 in India, compared to 1:1 in the U.S., in this prosaic example. That's what I mean when I say that it's really hard to find things out and get basic things done.

In this situation, I was able to use the over-the-top infrastructure of the luxury hotel to compensate for the vacuum of both available information and the means of actually procuring the ice pack. Similarly, the absence of trust means that folks either must spend time and money to reassure themselves about mundane things, or must simply avoid doing them. For the average resident of Chennai, compensating for such institutional inadequacies is utterly impractical.

When you can't get things done easily, you retreat to the familiar, the tried-and-trusted, to keep things simple. Rather than go the extra mile to find something with difficulty, or to engage with someone you don't really know, you simply end up avoiding things altogether. It's hard to tap into possibilities. The familiarity, comfort, and mutual understanding that come with repeated engagement fail to blossom. Trust is stillborn.

Sometimes, working with people we trust can help us sidestep such barriers to getting things done. Often, though, the absence of the "trust lubricant" merely aggravates the difficulties caused by a generally limited infrastructure. It's not hard to see that, in such circumstances, building an enterprise in Beijing, Bangalore, or Bujumbura is not like building a Facebook app in the comfort of a Harvard dorm. Entrepreneurs in Boston, like the scientists at the Wyss lab, have the luxury of a support system—both the result and the cause of ambient trust—that is tuned to propel their enterprises forward. Those of us working amid the institutional vacuums of the developing world lack this support.

There Is a Solution

In the 1970s, as an impressionable preteen in India, I saw a tear-jerker of a Hindi movie, *Toofan aur Deeya,* loosely translated as "Candle in the Storm." The title song of the movie stayed with me over the ages, and I internalized its allegorical message of a lonely candle flame spreading light and hope, however minimally, while being engulfed by a raging storm that threatened always to snuff it out. The movie's message was somewhat hackneyed, I admit. Yet it was nonetheless effective. Over the years, it has reminded me that we shouldn't underestimate the power of individual initiative, even against insurmountable odds. And the odds surely seem stacked against a creative individual seeking to solve a problem while enveloped by an institutionally weak and low-trust environment. But, better than pointing accusatory fingers at incompetent governments, or blaming the venality of corrupt individuals, we can take a page out of the actions of so many right around us in the developed world.

· · ·

Craig Newmark, for example, founder of the eponymous and now hugely popular online classified ads site Craigslist.org, remarked recently, uncannily echoing my childhood memory of a valiant candle flame: "Better to light a candle than to fight the darkness."[8] He used an old saying to reflect on the general problem of how we can find credible information in society.

Craigslist started when Newmark, having lost his job in 1995 just as the internet was taking off, decided to use his severance money to create a website that connected folks who were buying and selling things in the San Francisco area. Today, on his site, you can post ads for nanny services, jewelry, trucks, music gigs, and virtually anything else that occurs to you. It's mostly free, though the few services for which one pays are sufficient to make the enterprise insanely profitable.

Of course, Newmark must always have been obsessed with the idea that offers hosted on his site should have some authenticity to them so that transacting partners would come to trust it viscerally. This idea of trustworthy information appears to have stayed with him in the two decades since the site's launch. Today, his philanthropy is directed to backing entrepreneurs combating fake information, such as organizations that call out fake information in the news. Indeed, it certainly stays with you when a speech is rated "Liar, Liar, Pants on Fire" or labeled as maximally false with "Three Pinocchios," referring to the wooden puppet whose nose lengthens when he lies in Carlo Collodi's tale from the 1880s, *The Adventures of Pinocchio*.

Fake news has acquired new salience in the era of current U.S. President Donald Trump, who subscribes to his own alternate reality while accusing mainstream media of misrepresentation. Yet poor information is a societal problem, not only a Trump-era problem, and demands a societal response. And I think Newmark, with his support of creative entrepreneurs, is on to something. What, after all, are the alternatives? Moral exhortation? Of course, we should take every opportunity to remind ourselves of "thou shalt not lie" type of mandates, but one would not have to be cynical to question whether this action is enough. We can police lies, but there are simply too many being uttered these days to sanction by using laws, ostracism, fines, and so on.

· · ·

It helps that organizations in the business of verifying the credibility of information have often become viable. In other words, entrepreneurs can succeed by explicitly compensating for the absence of trust. Think of financial analysts who routinely grill executives when their companies put out overly optimistic plans and cause capital to be moved from those making less-plausible assertions to more-credible entities.

My favorite example of organizations in this genre is the *Consumer Reports* magazine and website, go-to places for millions of Americans to ascertain the quality of something, anything, they're about to buy—whether it be a dishwasher or a car or services of contractors to check out the quality of a new house. *Consumer Reports* runs fifty state-of-the-art laboratories nationwide to test products and services they identify,[9] free of any influence from the producers, since they're funded by subscriptions to their reports. It then issues no-holds-barred recommendations about the pros and cons of various offers, which are completely trusted by the market.

Like Craigslist, the magazine's origins go back to the entrepreneurial efforts of two individuals, in this case an Amherst College economics professor back in 1936 and his partner engineer with a background in product testing. The organization's success today in harnessing the trust that consumers have in it to police mischief is the result of decades of evolution and experimentation. Today, other than its core service of testing, it also engages in extensive research and even advocacy. It has lost some sway to newish organizations such as Yelp, an online website that reviews local businesses via crowdsourcing, though the lessons of *Consumer Reports'* trustworthy assessments remain.

Ironically, during the hysteria in the United States against communism, starting in the late 1930s, *Consumer Reports*, seen as favoring the little guy against corporations, was even investigated by the U.S. House Un-American Activities Committee. How ironic! But what could be more American than its entrepreneur founders' provision of reliable information to support free markets?

These few examples from the developed world suggest that the solution to the problem caused by mistrust usually lies ultimately with the insights of an individual entrepreneur. After all, even celebrated entities began as the actions of an entrepreneur. Take the iconic entrepreneur Sam Walton and his founding of Walmart. Walton sought to compensate for the missing retail infrastructure in what was then small-town America—indeed, very much like the developing country settings I consider here. Ultimately, he earned the trust of tens of millions of Americans who could reliably find affordable merchandise in thousands of hitherto inaccessible locations. Today's Walmart-like behemoths are, ultimately, the results of a brilliant entrepreneurial insight, magnified by problem solving over decades by Sam Walton's teams, which have amassed a track record of exhibiting admirable grit and persistence. It is time, I believe, for such entrepreneurs to step into the voids of the developing world.

Entrepreneurs in the Developing World

These days, most of the developing world lacks such credibility-enhancers. One solution is to encourage their creation. They could then ensure would-be and rightly skeptical buyers that a seller's representations are credible. There's a lot of room for creativity in this endeavor. Such an entity can be specific to certain needs or can be all-encompassing. It might make money for its owners or simply run as a social service. And it will usually employ technology. Creating such an organization is the perfect task for a would-be entrepreneur. As a consumer, I believe the organization will solve the low-trust problem I have with the mostly fly-by-night operators out to make a quick buck, with no recourse for me in the event that I feel shortchanged. I can't truly rely on self-serving promotional material from the purveyors of products, nor on equally self-serving industry associations, lobbying bodies, and such. And I am less concerned with debating which comes first—trust, or trust-enhancing institutions. Both are part of the effort to improve the conditions for problem solving. The credibility-enhancing organization created by our clever entrepreneur will itself have to earn the trust it seeks to spread, just as *Consumer Reports* has done.

This entrepreneur-centered solution is more general than the idea of creating a credibility-enhancer, however. After all, there are gaps in the developing world, other than unreliable information that prevents folks from getting together. Even if I partner with someone, based on credible information, I might still want to contractually reassure myself that we both have face-saving ways out if things sour. That requires good legal services, another factor mostly missing in the developing world—a gap that might make me shy away from taking an otherwise good deal. In addition, if I had access to a low-cost loan, I might be able to afford to buy some equipment that helps me save more over time than the up-front cost of the equipment. So the absence of low-cost debt, too, can impede creativity. Many more trust voids of this nature exist in the developing world. But on the flip side of these gaps is the view that they represent opportunities for proactive action.

If you stop to think about it, we take a lot for granted when we whip out our smartphones to accomplish many everyday tasks. Standing in a store, we may check whether a product might be available more cheaply elsewhere and then, with a wave in front of a scanner, possibly ensure that money is seamlessly transferred from a bank account to a merchant who will quickly ship our product. Missing intermediaries in developing countries often prevent this from happening. Without these intermediaries, individuals are prevented by absence of information, contracts, funds, and what-have-you from coming together.

Indeed, the evolution of money transactions online in both the developed and the developing worlds demonstrates these concepts in action. PayPal, for example, built a large enterprise in the developed world by reassuring consumers that online payments were secure. Alipay in China, part of the Alibaba group of enterprises, and PayTM in India are en route to accomplishing a similar feat. These developed and developing world successes show that addressing the problem of mistrust can productively move societies forward significantly.

Entrepreneurs like Craig Newmark in the San Francisco Bay Area can build entities to compensate for these trust limitations, contribute to society, and make a buck while doing so. Indeed, virtually all the reputable entities that I can think of in the developing world have worked assiduously to cultivate precisely such trust. They've realized that to reassure their constituents and well-wishers, they need to go the extra mile to compensate for the low-trust, low-infrastructure environments within which they typically operate.

. . .

One of my favorite examples is the world's largest NGO, or nongovernmental organization, one that you most likely have never heard of: BRAC. The awkward acronym originally stood for Bangladesh Rehabilitation Assistance Committee. But BRAC now also stands for "Building Resources Across Communities."[10] It was founded in Bangladesh in 1971 to rehabilitate victims of a devastating cyclone, around the same time as a civil war that resulted in the country's separation as a nation-state from Pakistan.[11] When the cyclone hit in 1970, Fazle Hasan Abed, then thirty-four years old, had been working as chief accountant for Shell Oil, Bangladesh, a coveted position with an enviable salary. He realized that the devastation wrought by the cyclone had presented him with a life-changing moment. He recently described his memories in this manner:

> I saw trees uprooted and so on. But we never realized the extent of damage in the offshore islands of Bangladesh and the shore areas. Within two days, news started coming in from outside, and we thought we needed to do something about it. So I mobilized a speedboat from Shell Oil, and some oil, some kerosene and matches and utensils, food and so on, which we took to remote offshore islands where they lost everything. . . . The scene was just horrendous—bodies strewn everywhere—humans, animals, everything. That shocked me to an extent that I felt that the kind of life I led hardly had any meaning in the context in which these people lived—the fragility of life of poor people.

By 1971, Abed had left his position at Shell to found BRAC with the goal of fighting poverty. Rather than focusing on one problem at a time, BRAC recognized that poverty stems from an interconnected web of issues. Over the years, it has evolved into taking a more holistic approach. Indeed, BRAC found that topics as diverse as healthcare, education, finance, and more are all linked to poverty. Yet, to achieve any of its goals BRAC had to find its way in a country that in most respects was brand new and starting from scratch. In other words, saying that the NGO faced a country with infrastructure and trust limitations is a huge understatement. Indeed, for the most part, BRAC faced a situation in which there was *no* infrastructure whatsoever.

Time and again, BRAC responded by creating the trust-enabling infrastructure itself—creating the conditions necessary to create solutions to the problem of poverty. Speaking about the limitations of addressing any one problem, however critical, Abed has remarked:

We've always considered [microfinance] as one part of a solution, and [it] must be combined with many other things to improve the lives of poor people. For example, if a woman gets money to buy a cow, and then she gets milk but can't sell it, you haven't really helped her very much. So you have to create a market for her to sell the milk. This is microcredit "plus." The other "plus" you have to provide is healthcare and education for children, because if children remain uneducated, this poverty is going to reproduce in the next generation. So you have to do microcredit "plus-plus" to really address the concerns of poor people. Many in the development community are not geared toward this. Most organizations want to do one thing well. I don't mind that, but then they aren't dealing with poverty as a whole.

In other words, whenever BRAC saw a gap in the infrastructure, the organization worked to fill that gap, all the while developing a wide variety of programs and initiatives. From these efforts, everyone has internalized that there is no showstopper for BRAC. Its team of entrepreneurs simply would not be deterred by the seemingly endless obstacles it faced. As a result, BRAC earned yet more trust. BRAC's near half-century of growth teaches us that creating strong infrastructure enables entrepreneurship. Infrastructure begets trust. Trust begets creativity and problem solving. I call this *creating the conditions to create.*

To further reassure its various partners, BRAC's monitoring unit measured everything thoroughly, from the success and failure of all the programs to developing myriad measures of societal impact. BRAC returned unspent money to its donors, underpromising and overdelivering on its obligations. If its employees saw a social problem, they were encouraged to try to innovate and work to alleviate it. The more that employees trusted that their work produced tangible results for society in the tough "game" that is poverty reduction, the more BRAC was able to recruit top talent and further maintain its trustworthy reputation.

Employee-led and -nurtured creativity over the decades has led to a stream of productive efforts. Some, such as legal aid for impoverished Bangladeshi migrant workers in the Middle East, and work on women's rights, aren't financially self-sustaining. Yet others, like some attempts at retail marketing, or investments in mobile money transfer entities (the last in conjunction with the Gates Foundation and the IFC, both entities that trust BRAC), are robustly profitable, and serve to finance other parts of the BRAC system. Over the years I've been struck by BRAC's emphasis on harnessing creativity and entrepreneurship to address problems, rather than on determining whether there's money to be made on a particular venture, as long as the entirety is financially robust. Indeed, about two-thirds of BRAC's budget now comes from internally generated profits, as opposed to the exclusive reliance it placed on donations at its inception.

Now in his eighties, Sir Fazle Abed told me that when BRAC announced its desire to expand its operations into Africa, donors virtually tripped over themselves to support it, so great was the trust the organization inspires. Today, BRAC operates in a dozen challenging countries in Africa and South Asia.

• • •

The general lesson of this introduction, then, is that even gutsy and creative entrepreneurs like those discussed here can't merely set out to create. In the developing world, they must *create the conditions to create*. And the foremost condition entrepreneurs must create is to find and cultivate whatever it takes to induce trust, from their talent, their partners, their clients, and others. This idea may sound unconventional. In fact, its imperatives are rather onerous. It puts a lot on the shoulders of the beleaguered would-be entrepreneur. But I think it's in fact the most practical approach.

Those of us focused on the developing world lack the support system to propel enterprise forward. We could simply wait for the law, or the state, to solve the problems. But the law is too often compromised in the developing world. And the state is weakened by the very infrastructure-depleted and low-trust environment it is ostensibly meant to address.

Meanwhile, prevailing scarcity in developing countries—for clean water, for energy, for adequate healthcare, for scarce spots in universities, for you-name-it—complicates things because it often induces a winner-take-all scramble for scraps. Thomas Hobbes, writing in *Leviathan* in 1651, famously described such life as "nasty, brutish and short."[12] This truth is precisely why we must find a way to encourage behavior that is its polar opposite—reassuring people, weaving a web of trust that fosters the risk-taking that is creativity's handmaiden.

Why This Matters Today

If ever there were a time that addressing problems of economic and social inclusion was relevant, that time is now. Those left behind don't trust those in control to focus on their needs. The consequences of having a large disenfranchised population loom all around us. Look at the disaffected voters kicking the United Kingdom out of the European Union, or the unlikely rise of impresario Donald Trump.

You see pockets of deprivation everywhere, including closer to where I live in the developed world, which is subject to the same ravages of distrust as anywhere. A recent contaminated water crisis in Flint, Michigan, was the sort of episode—poisoned water, corrupt politicians, complicit local media, even children with mental illness—that we see in several developing countries. The repair of that torn institutional fabric will challenge us for some time to come.

You also see underdevelopment of a different sort in pockets of the developed world. These aren't, however, without their charms. As an Indian seeking spicy cuisine, I frequently wander into India-towns and Chinatowns in cities around the developed world to satisfy my cravings. Anyone who has done so sees bustling enterprise in an ecosystem that often parallels that of the mainstream that it abuts. It's functional and typified by informal ways of addressing the trust issue. But it is not a system that permits enterprises to scale easily into the size of Walmart. That requires BRAC-like attention to systematically addressing the infrastructural gaps.

Flint-like disasters and Chinatown-like settings aside, the vast majority of the five billion of the world's seven billion people who live outside the economic mainstream, eking out a subsistence existence, live in the developing world. Their problems are now yours and mine. Witness recent years' teeming masses propelling themselves through unspeakable hazards onto Europe's shores from the conflict-ravaged Middle East.

Some will say that the developed world has already contributed aid to the developing world for decades to cater to these disenfranchised. And they will say that this commitment was amplified by a focus on the so-called Millennium Development Goals set at a U.N. summit in 2000. This is true. Indeed, we are living at a time when average poverty levels are at the lowest they've been in a long time, helped along by rising incomes in populous China and, to some extent, in India. As the Harvard psychology professor Steven Pinker reminds us, we're also living in a rather peaceable time overall, notwithstanding the heartrending images that often appear on our newspapers' front pages and our TV screens—an argument he makes based on data such as the total number of wars fought around the world and the number of battle deaths globally.[13]

My intent here is not to denigrate this progress. Rather, it's to recognize that there's more to be done, and more efficiently, even as these average levels clearly mask considerable differences in individuals' experiences. For example, the disparity between haves and have-nots in virtually every major country in the world has increased. That rankles.

In the class I teach at Harvard filled with impressionable and idealistic undergraduates, two approaches to economic development come up frequently. As one student put it to me last year, it's easy to be seduced by the tug-at-your-heartstrings and shame-you-into-action approach of giving more aid, supplemented by analytical assurance that the reason we haven't achieved more is not that what we're doing is misguided, it's that we haven't done nearly enough of it. This is an approach sometimes associated with the economist Jeff Sachs in New York.[14]

His colleague William Easterly, also a New York City economist, has taken Sachs to task for what he calls misguided, utopian paternalism. Easterly denounces Sachs's view as a delusion, a modern version of what the English poet Rudyard Kipling called the "White Man's Burden," the idea that outsiders from the developed world can swoop in and solve local problems in poorer locales. He'd rather spur individual problem-solving activity locally in developing countries.[15]

In a sense, Easterly and others emphasizing individual agency do not go far enough. Exhortations don't suffice. I hope to show in this book that what separates attempts at local entrepreneurship that *truly* move societies forward from the overwhelming majority (whose effect is creditable but more piecemeal) is that the former manage to *create the conditions to create*. The success stories

I present will consciously, perhaps even inadvertently, provide infrastructural solutions that do not help only them but help others, as well.

Yet I also think that Easterly is wrong to denigrate Sachs. Aid is super-important for the bottom at the bottom, for example, where people have virtually no capacity to help themselves. The problem is not the lack of aid; rather, it's the low-trust environment within which some aid is being dispensed. Hypothetically, if donors could trust that aid, rather than being misused, will achieve its stated purpose of allowing human beings to develop fully, I can't imagine that Easterly or anyone else would object.

This brings us back to the core of the solution I'm advocating: Whether entrepreneurs pursue an aid-based approach, a more self-help approach, or something in between, they need to find ways to cultivate trust. To do this, entrepreneurs must learn to *create the conditions to create.*

. . .

Examples of entrepreneurs exploring this kind of trust building can be seen all throughout the developing world, from BRAC in Bangladesh to efforts in China and India and Brazil and Mexico. Such entrepreneurs fill the vacuums of trust left by dysfunctional institutions in myriad ways. Their stories, which I chronicle here for you, the reader, have taught me much. Both community-based low-tech solutions and newfangled high-tech solutions work to create a cocoon of trust. But doing so requires a mindset that embraces the fundamental point that, to build their enterprises at scale, it's insufficient for entrepreneurs to focus solely on the problem they seek to address—they must also address the ambient inadequacies within which the problem resides. It's often easier to do so if one seeks out preexisting informal structures of society that are already functional, rather than creating entirely new ones.

Cookie-cutter recipes to address complex issues are hard to find in life, though fostering trust, so as to *create the conditions to create*, comes awfully close to such a solution.

One

The Why's and How's of Trust

Comparing the dairy industries of China and India reveals the why's and how's of trust. Why? Because trust weaves together in a web all those needed for productive enterprise—and because, when this web is torn, there's a dramatic fall from grace. How? There are many ways to weave this web of trust, even in the same prosaic context—the production of milk. The Chinese solution emphasizes speed and high technology. In this chapter, I profile an entrepreneur borrowing tricks from California's technology industry to make his cows "happy"—while the Indian solution is a slow-but-rock-solid, community-based solution developed over decades and anchoring the future. The disparate entrepreneurial paths to the same high-productivity goal share the emphasis on trust that cocoons everyone, from dairy farmer to end consumer.

Rebuilding Lost Trust

In 2008, anxious parents in Gansu Province, deep in the Chinese mainland, began visiting hospitals with their ailing infants. Tests found that several domestic brands of dairy-based infant formula powders they were consuming contained melamine, an industrial chemical used in plastics and fertilizers that can cause kidney failure in small children.[1] Ultimately six babies died and approximately 300,000 were affected during what became known as "the Chinese milk scandal."[2]

Somewhere along the supply chain, intermediaries had been diluting raw milk with water and then adding melamine to fool quality tests (melamine is high in nitrogen, and most tests only look at nitrogen levels as a proxy for protein levels). In some cases, dairy farmers themselves engaged in this practice, with the tacit approval of big dairy companies like Sanlu, to squeeze out some extra profits in an industry with very low margins.

Despite government efforts to restrict negative media coverage during that summer's Beijing Olympics, the scandal caused international outrage. Protests and lawsuits followed. The government eventually tried the chairwoman of Sanlu and sentenced her to life in prison. Two wholesalers were convicted of overseeing the dilution and contamination and then selling the contaminated products with full knowledge of the health risks—and they were actually executed in November 2009. These were unusual moves, since the government rarely cracks down so hard on bad actors in the food industry.

Indeed, this milk crisis was hardly the first instance in which food contamination threatened the health of the Chinese. There was the episode a few years back when farmers' use of chemicals to accelerate growth resulted in a rash of watermelon explosions.[3] Earlier in 2015, authorities found so-called "zombie beef" in the supply chain. Certain vendors had somehow gotten access to forty-year-old beef that had been thawed and refrozen many times over and were selling it across China.[4]

And then there was the discovery in March 2013 of more than 16,000 dead pigs floating in a tributary of the Huangpu River, a significant source of Shanghai's drinking water.[5] China Central Television reported that pig farmers in Zhejiang Province were selling pigs that had died of disease or natural causes to black market dealers, who then butchered them and illegally sold the pork. After a few of these malfeasants were sentenced to life in prison, the lucrative illegal trade in dead pigs plummeted, and farmers started dumping them in rivers in droves, instead of paying to discard them in pits. The images of masked and suited sanitation workers hauling the bloated carcasses out of the river with poles and nets repulsed the residents of Shanghai.[6]

Even so, the tainted milk crisis was different. It struck a deeper chord. Why?

That crisis affected mostly young children and infants. Due to China's long-standing one-child policy, there is an entire generation of parents who have invested all their hopes and energy into their single child. They are thus willing to go to greater lengths and expense to protect him or her: After the news broke, many parents undertook shelf-clearing expeditions to buy and bring back expensive foreign-brand infant formula from New Zealand, Singapore, and Hong Kong. Years later, this pattern continues.[7]

This response neatly captures the net result of the scandal: Many Chinese simply don't trust their domestic private food sector anymore. A trust vacuum exists.

This trust vacuum creates a vicious cycle, one that's difficult to break. The problem stems from all sides in the dairy industry. For example, the price-sensitivity of consumers who are mostly not wealthy drives down prices for companies trying to win the market. This dynamic means that dairy farmers get low prices for their raw milk. If they are to make any profit at all, they have to lower their costs. For a small farmer wrapped up in the myriad daily challenges of running a dairy operation, the most expedient thing to do is to cut corners. Even if a farmer tries to take the high road—by investing in higher-quality feed for his cows, for example—and to recoup his costs by selling milk at a higher premium, it won't pay off easily. Most consumers wouldn't place any faith in his efforts, at least not for a while. This lack of trust persists because the level of trust in *all* dairy producers has become so vanishingly small.

In reality, many different players and methods can be involved with rebuilding trust. But rather than waiting for others to solve the problem, the entrepreneur can be the change agent herself. Her solution may be a tech solution. Or it might harness the community. Or both. She will almost certainly have to reimagine the role of talent, to attract it to an industry now perceived as staid and boring.

Filling the Trust Vacuum

Even when the government does try to solve the trust problem through new regulations and consoling announcements, these initiatives do not always work quickly enough. Entrepreneurs waiting for others to provide solutions to the trust vacuum are likely to be waiting quite a while.

For example, in China, when the melamine milk scandal surfaced in 2008 the government sought to contain the mounting outrage from parents of sick children. Wen Jiabao, then the nation's premier, who cultivates a studiedly avuncular image, tried to apologize publicly. This is rare, since Chinese leaders are usually obsessed with projecting strength. However, despite their infrequent deployment, these apologies are a key part of Chinese political theater—a technique for managing the "optics" of delicate situations, a pressure valve to let off some steam without conceding too much.

"As the head of the government, I feel extremely guilty," Wen said in September of that year. "I sincerely apologize to all of you. What we are doing now is to ensure that nothing like this will ever happen again, and we are not only talking about milk. We will never let the same situation repeat with any kind of food product. Please trust us. We will strengthen quality control on new products to ensure that there will not be any more issues. Public confidence can only be rebuilt on merciless punishment."[8]

Yet today these pledges still ring hollow to many ordinary Chinese. After all, senior Chinese political figures had made similar promises in response to *other* food safety scandals. Critics asked how new regulations could be effective, as there weren't enough food safety inspectors to enforce them. Consumers signaled what they thought of these steps by purchasing imported milk powder products whenever they could.[9]

The combination of tighter regulations and harsh sentences doled out to accused perpetrators (including the execution of the head of China's Food and Drug Administration in 2007)[10] seemed to have improved the situation. The government's new rules have had the effect of driving many smaller, "backyard" dairy producers out of business, encouraging consolidation into larger farms. This has made testing and rejection of low-quality milk much easier.

Still, ordinary Chinese continue to distrust their food as being unsafe. Beyond the dairy sector, food contamination problems continue to this day. The public's trust in its food remains broken.

• • •

So much for government remedies. Another set of attempts may emanate from activists.

In 2011, Wu Heng launched a website called "Throw It Out the Window," featuring an interactive map based on crowd-sourced information about food scandals around the country. It soon went viral—and quickly crashed from too much traffic.[11] Give Wu credit for showing initiative.

Wu's website has to contend with two powerful forces.[12] One is the Communist Party, which is intent on maintaining order and has often intervened swiftly to curtail activists protesting such issues as pollution or human rights violations. If Wu oversteps, he will be similarly sanctioned;[13] if he underreports, his enterprise lacks credibility. It is a tenuous existence.

The other obstacle, perhaps even more daunting, is what Wu has called food safety fatigue. He thinks people have learned to just live with the risk and worries that his website has simply had the effect of desensitizing consumers to the dangers of contaminated food. He cites the high prices of certified organic alternatives. Furthermore, the cumulative health effects of eating polluted or contaminated food could take years to materialize in the average person.[14] This combination, indeed, is the magic recipe for resignation.

Resignation is an adaptive strategy present in many communities around the developing world. In India, for example, the Hindi phrase *chalta hai* is a pervasive response to such problems. Functionally meaning "it's okay, let's carry on," it is often used to condone cutting corners, breaking rules, looking the other way. This resignation holds a certain logic for the poor, or even for the middle classes living in societies plagued by corruption or hampered by dysfunctional institutions. When the vicissitudes of life are so random and often cruel, the only choice left is to simply decide not to be bothered by them.

In other words, outrage is a luxury many low-income consumers feel they can ill afford. So they throw up their hands, and say, *Mei ban fa*—"Nothing can be done."

Wu Heng's website showed pervasive mistrust. It was a good step in the direction of finding a solution, though it was not remotely enough.[15]

. . .

Of course, many solutions have been tried, and many have failed to rebuild trust in China's dairy industry. But the *mei ban fa* attitude, while completely understandable, does not help, either. There is *plenty* to be done.

In an unlikely move to fill the trust vacuum, an entrepreneur named Charles Shao has brought his education as an engineer from California's elite universities, and his experience building a tech company—ultimately sold to Google for a handsome sum—to the "Wild East" of the dairy industry in China.[16] Shao is compact and stocky, with an informal, laid-back manner that—along with the top two buttons left open on his shirt—evokes his youth spent in California. He speaks with a kind of soft-spoken bluntness. When asked about his core challenges, he smiles and shrugs in a way that suggests he has indeed assessed the height of the mountain he's trying to climb as a dairy farmer in China, and he has come away impressed yet undaunted.

"It's a basic consumer education problem," he says. "If you can afford it, you buy the international brand of infant formula. It's a no-brainer. It's something you can trust. The melamine scandal turned things upside down." Shao noted that the melamine crisis galvanized the government, and its harsh penalties had some effect on cleaning up the supply chain: "Melamine is gone; it's a lot better now." But he points out that a much larger problem persists, seven years later. "Consumer confidence in milk in China is so low today that there is a lot of foreign milk in China that is two or three times—one is even ten times—the average price. But people will pay money for it."

How can a lone entrepreneur overcome the suspicions of a billion cost-conscious food shoppers and inspire trust, despite being in this vacuum, devoid of confidence? His mind naturally gravitates to his strong suit, technology. This is what he's relied on from the time he started Huaxia Dairy Farm just outside Beijing in 2004, well before the onset of the melamine crisis.

The Beginnings of a High-Tech, Happy-Cow Solution in Chinese Dairy

At Huaxia's inception, Shao had the sense that China lagged decades behind the United States. in terms of its dairy productivity. He saw an opportunity to bring U.S. standards into the industry. But he had no background in farming or food. So why agribusiness?

"No one is into agriculture in a serious way here," he responds.

By "serious," Shao means there is no competitor who is serious about innovation, particularly about reimagining the use of technology in this otherwise staid setting. For example, from the outset, Shao worked to improve the gene pool of China's dairy herd. Cows in China produce relatively low quantities of milk. So Shao started by building a herd of high-quality imported and crossbred cows. He used new data management systems to construct advanced facilities, sourced high-quality feed, and installed the latest equipment. He went way beyond what Chinese regulations required, meeting U.S. Food and Drug Administration standards for processing.

Although these decisions raised Shao's costs 15 percent over those of his competitors, he felt that the investment would pay off quickly: He would produce more and better milk per head, lose fewer cows to sickness, cut down labor costs, and have to replace equipment less often. The goal was to emphasize quality, a strategy that would be well worth the higher costs.

"When I first came [back to China], these people were thinking the cow was just a machine to produce milk," he says. This

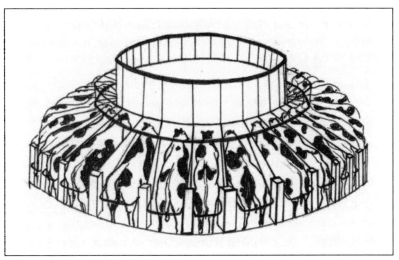

Technology applied at a Chinese dairy: multiple cows being milked simultaneously.

attitude led to low output. Good dairy farmers will tell you that happy cows produce more milk. "I did a lot of research and development on cow comfort," he remarks.

At the farm he built outside Beijing in 2013, these efforts show. A specially engineered "water curtain" circulates cool air throughout the barn. Some cows move freely around their barn enclosures; most lie on their sides and happily munch on feed. They are basically lounging around, completely relaxed. "How do you tell a cow is happy?" Shao asks. "She sits down and chews her cud, then regurgitates it." Electric golf carts drive up and down, moving the feed closer so the herd can eat without getting up.

"If a cow moves from my 2004 farm to this one," Shao points out, referring to the first facility that he built without these amenities, "I get five liters more milk [daily] per cow. She eats more, relaxes more, and gives more milk."

The facility doesn't have the stench one conventionally encounters on dairy farms, either. Cows amble out of the milking barn, and mechanical sweepers and flowing water continuously remove the manure they drop. The manure is then piped to another building, where it will be processed into organic fertilizer to be sold to other farms.

Charles Shao views his role as one focused not solely on his own business but on the health of the industry as a whole. In the same way that he improved on the dirty, unventilated barns he found on arrival back in his home country, Shao sees a key part of his role as an entrepreneur as improving the entire ecosystem of dairy farming in China. He also did something unusual: He started partnerships with U.S. veterinary colleges to train Chinese dairy professionals. He worked with other dairies, helping them import better feed from the United States, effectively training employees of competitors for free. "Without research and development, my business will not survive. But I can't do all the R&D on my own."

Some critics were puzzled, even angered by these moves. How, they wondered, could Shao expect to make money with higher costs? Chinese consumers would not be able to afford the more expensive milk, these critics argued. Moreover, why was Shao not protecting his innovations and ideas? "My investors worry that if I train my competitors I'll go out of business," he says. They plead with him, saying he's basically giving his intellectual property away. How dare he share these ideas with others—with *competitors*—encouraging competition that could doom his business and possibly further hurt an industry already on the ropes?

This idea of sharing information with the competition—even valuable information—did not originate with Charles Shao, however. It borrows from the technology industry's "open-source" movement, in which everyone in the industry freely accesses the knowledge of others and contributes to enhancing it. In other words, people "pay it forward," trusting that others will do likewise. It's hard for the Chinese dairy entrepreneurs to appreciate this, however, stuck in a low-trust environment as they are.

Shao's version of "open-source" for dairy was to train farmers in his region for free. Free! He felt that his compatriots, thus educated, would be in a position to contribute themselves. Down the road, this upgrading of skill sets will win back the consumer's confidence in Chinese dairy.

"If the quality of an entire industry has improved, then all companies in the industry have a better environment for development," Shao explains. "If I am the only person doing sustainability forever, the business stops if I stop. If I can influence other people to do it the way I do it, my average cost will be lower." Giving away knowledge, he argues, "actually increases my competitive edge. You have to keep improving yourself, otherwise people will catch up."

Sure it's risky. But what isn't? There are huge risks to operating within the status quo in the dairy world: If his competitors are found to be producing contaminated or low-quality milk, he'll be lumped in with them, no matter what he does. In Shao's view, it's risky not to take this risk.

Call it "going the extra mile," call it "enlightened self-interest"—whatever else it may be, it's a longer-term, patient play. Shao is planting the seeds of a harvest he hopes to reap when, as he believes, the Chinese dairy industry will boom due to new-found trust and he will be one of its major players.

In Homer's *Odyssey*, Odysseus sails past creatures known as the Sirens, who sing bewitching songs that draw sailors off course and lead to shipwrecks. Odysseus knows the nature of the danger ahead, however, and commands his crew to tie him to the mast of the boat and plug their own ears so that they will not be tempted to steer off-course to certain ruin.

Odysseus' idea of an irreversible commitment in the form of "binding oneself to the mast" has many modern manifestations. Some of my academic economist colleagues devised a commitment savings product called SEED (Save, Earn, Enjoy Deposits) that was a form of forced saving for women in the Philippines. It helped the women sidestep the problem of not having control over the family budget—the men in the family would otherwise often squander money that could otherwise be saved—and also helped them bypass self-control problems. SEED produced the desired result in just one year.[17] Charles Shao, by committing publicly to his open-source approach for raising milk quality, has similarly constrained himself so that he is not tempted to cut corners, sell lower-quality milk, and perpetuate the Chinese milk industry's low-trust problem.

Shao's borrowing from his technology background did not end with the idea of "open-source." He often talks, for instance, about the "Intel Inside" campaign, which helped that semiconductor computer chip maker become a household name and a highly successful company—even though no one ever walked into a retail store and bought an Intel chip. Still, almost every PC that consumers bought had Intel chips inside. Consequently, most consumers came to know the brand "Intel." Shao is using this same strategy with Yoplait, the multinational yogurt giant.

Indeed, Shao's biggest bet isn't on retail sales to consumers. Rather, it is in selling his milk to huge companies such as General Mills, which owns the Yoplait brand. Precisely like Intel inside PCs, Shao wants Huaxia milk to be the brand inside the Yoplait products sold in China. "We've been selected as the only farm that can provide quality milk and be an environmentally complying company in China. I hope that my capacity can grow with Yoplait. They need more milk; I can build more farms for them." He sees cultivating trust as essential to this partnership level, too. "With Yoplait, we have worked with their people for the last seven years. Häagen-Dazs never built a Chinese plant because of the 'made in China' problem. These large companies require this trust building. They can afford to wait. Now they [Yoplait] know us well enough, and they want to move forward."

In this way, Shao progresses in his quest to build trust in the entire system. If a company as large as Yoplait has determined that Shao's milk is desirable and trustworthy—that a milk brand from China is desirable and trustworthy for the nation's consumers—then the industry as a whole will benefit. Moreover, other customers in China will look at the Huaxia brand with greater trust.

• • •

Technology has played a starring role in Shao's reinvention of Chinese dairy. In fact, it has many more possibilities, though also numerous limitations.

As an example, in the wake of the melamine scandal, Shao looked to technology as his default solution. He focused on developing a traceability system, so milk could be tracked back to the individual cow and farm that produced it. "Right now, traceability only starts at a processing plant in China. They don't know anything before that. In the U.S. [it is pretty much the same, but] because the infrastructure is good, you don't need to trace individual cows. So innovation in farming is very limited because of that." Since the infrastructure in China isn't as good, Shao needs to be both more creative and more ambitious, which in this case entails going beyond the best practices in the American dairy industry.

Shao has been moving quickly—starting from 180 cows, Huaxia's dairy has grown to over 20,000 cows—and going all-in on technology. Five days after a Huaxia cow is born, it is tagged with a radio frequency identification chip behind its ear. Every time it enters the milking room, this chip is scanned, calling up its health history and milk yield data. Employees can pinpoint problems and can link the milk in a given batch with an individual cow that contributed to it.

Yet technology alone isn't enough to cement this new reputation, for either Huaxia or the industry. Shao has also focused on building a brand with consumers. In 2006, the company started selling what's translated as Wondermilk, a product it marketed as "100 percent natural, safe, and pasteurized." After some key endorsements from high-profile Chinese celebrities, its sales soared. This occurred two years before the melamine scandal.

"Wondermilk was meant to be a showcase, used as an advertisement," Shao says. "It's a symbol, a message to put out there. The consumer will say, 'Anything made in China is no good.' People ask me all the time: 'The pollution is so bad, the air is so bad, so how clean is your milk?' That trust issue becomes a debate, always." Wondermilk sales are a small fraction of Huaxia's revenue, but Shao sees it as a key element of building trust in his own brand, and in the larger "brand" of the Chinese dairy industry, as well.

And there remains a rather large unsolved problem where technology is likely to play a starring role. Shao has trouble convincing young talent that the dairy industry is trendy and "cool." Most see life on a dairy farm as something to escape. The talent issue is especially tough in the context of China's demography. Thanks to its one-child policy, China is, on average, a much older country than India; in the latter, more than half the population is under the age of twenty-five. Young Chinese are racing toward the cities, not the countryside, so Shao has had a hard time finding workers.

"The social fabric is changing," he notes. "The younger people are living in apartments now. Once the older generation dies, no one will do that kind of work. I couldn't hire people to pick up corn stalks [used for feed] blown over by a windstorm last year. There is no one there anymore to do that work." His future success hinges in large part on whether he can position dairy farming as a lucrative, high-status realm of enterprise for ambitious young Chinese: Can he make dairy farming cool?

Even though others in China don't (yet) share these views, Shao is a congenital optimist. To take on this challenge, perhaps he has to be. "When I started, this was a business that no one wanted to get into," he remarks. "Dairy was very low-tech. Today that has changed. We have trained more than 3,000 people in the industry. The trend is a lot more professional people are coming into the business, and training others. On the farm level, it is still a problem. As we improve the technology, more people will come in. On my new farm near Shanghai, my average worker's age is less than thirty—I'm the oldest guy! We're getting more young people. We raised wages. Dairy farming has become a big thing in China. The profile has gone up; the pay is getting a lot better. A vet today gets paid six times more than he did ten years ago."

Despite this talent constraint, and perhaps fueled by his optimism, Shao is nothing if not a fast mover. In 2016, Huaxia merged with Saikexing, an Inner Mongolian dairy, to get to a combined dairy size of 130,000 cows, then the third largest in China. A year later, the herd size had more than doubled to 275,000 cows. With this platform, Shao's technologies might well move speedily across the rest of Chinese dairy.[18]

• • •

Charles Shao's solution to the dairy industry trust vacuum is to highlight quality by harnessing technology. Still, an analysis is necessary to determine if the quality signal truly works. Let us consider some other experiences in "food" writ large, some involving my Chinese students, others orchestrated by global companies.

Ma Juan is a Singapore-based professor at INSEAD, a global business school. From her hometown of Nanjing, she went on to study at the University of Toronto, then did research at Harvard, and now straddles the cultures of East and West quite comfortably. In the process, she has become an informed observer of China's food industry. Yet her wariness about what she herself chooses to eat mostly comes from personal experience.[19]

Ma Juan's mother is a trained chemist who runs a company that manufactures dyes for use in fabrics and industrial products. She has long known that greedy intermediaries use these dyes on food to fool their customers into paying higher prices. Indeed, this problem is especially prevalent in rice. Historically, purple rice was reserved for emperors, and for centuries rice with this color has fetched high prices. This trend of dyeing food frustrates Ma Juan's mother—since the 1970s, mandatory labels on her company's products have warned that the products are prohibited for use in foods—but there is little she can do to prevent unscrupulous food sellers from buying her firm's dyes once they are on the open market. But she can certainly do something about her own family's diet. So, for the past fifteen years or so, Ma Juan's mother has planted a sizable garden on a patch of land in a semi-urban part of Nanjing, near an industrial park, in order to have some control over her family's diet. Like Ma Juan's mother, many wealthy people in urban China have started growing their own food to protect their families' health. These moves have propelled Ma Juan to further study food safety in China.

In 2013, this interest led Ma Juan and a team of researchers from Harvard Business School (including myself as a team member) to go to Hangzhou to study this further. Originally famous for its picturesque West Lake, the city is now a burgeoning tech hub and home to the Chinese online behemoth Alibaba. We wanted to see how information about quality affected consumers' decisions in the wake of the milk scandal.

We worked with a domestic dairy producer called Beingmate, the largest domestic infant formula manufacturer in China.

Beingmate's products had been tested and found clean during the melamine scandal. It had invested heavily in traceability systems and had even obtained a key international quality certification. The company supported the idea of a randomized control trial—the gold standard for assessing interventions, inspired by long-standing practices in medicine—to test whether seeing this information on quality printed on product packaging would affect shoppers' behavior. To its credit, Beingmate took some risk: The results were to be made publicly available, whether it showed that their system worked or not.

The researchers set up three groups. The first treatment group shopped in supermarkets where the products were placed next to a simple card that read "Beingmate is the go-to brand for your babies." This is a common Beingmate advertising slogan. No other quality-related information was provided.

The second treatment group found the products next to a card that read "Beingmate provides a brand-new quality traceability system that achieves traceability from milk powders' raw material, production, marketing to sales."

And the third treatment group got the card with a notice that Beingmate had met an "international ISO quality certification." We Harvard researchers distributed these products with labels in eighty supermarkets around Hangzhou. Through all this, our idea was to explore how these notices affected consumers relative to a well-specified control group of consumers who were exposed to milk products with no additional information provided. Then our team sat back and watched people shop.

We tracked the sales, in both dollars and volume, of Beingmate products at every supermarket for three fourteen-day periods—before, during, and after the experiment. When we tallied up the results and compared using statistical analyses, we were astonished.

To our great surprise, we found that the more credible the information provided, the *lower* the sales! And this effect was stronger in higher-income areas than in lower-income districts. The negative dip in sales occurred not only for infant formula, but for *all* Beingmate products.

The researchers were shocked at this result. It ran counter to everything we had learned in our training as economists—all the theory that said that more information on high quality would increase demand and lead to more efficient markets, wherein responsible producers would be rewarded, and on and on. Instead, what seemed to be happening was that the labels redirected consumers' attention to the original scandals that necessitated them. And the more sophisticated and info-savvy the consumers, the more likely they were to be turned off by the whole effort.

The researchers named this dynamic the "reminder effect." In the end, these labels were not convincing anyone that the product was safe; all they were doing was *reminding* people of the intractable, off-putting problem of food contamination. It was almost as if the Chinese consumer could not cross some invisible but critical threshold of trust for these techniques to work, as they have been proven to work in wealthier markets like the United States or Europe. It was like a rocket's reaching escape velocity: If the rocket does not cross the threshold, it isn't going anywhere. In September 2008, right after the melamine scandal broke, Wen Jiabao had pleaded with the Chinese people to "trust us," but apparently nobody was buying it. Consumers' view of China's dairy industry was and is—like the milk itself, circa 2008—entirely too tainted.

Even more comprehensive efforts to foster trust may face the same issues. For example, the German retail giant Metro A.G. started a pilot program in Anhui Province in 2008, a province adjacent to Shanghai. Called Star Farm Consultancy, it guaranteed high-quality, fresh, safely packaged foods to wholesale buyers, as well as traceability to the point of origin. Metro's big-box stores stocked over 100 of these certified items. But replication of the program in other provinces was compromised by questions about the customers' willingness to pay for these "extras."[20]

The U.S. consumer takes for granted the credibility—and value—of the U.S. Department of Agriculture seal of approval. That little USDA sticker means something to the person browsing in the meat aisle—if a product has made it past the inspectors, then most likely it's safe to eat. But in China, people don't seem to believe sufficiently in the information provided to be willing to pay for the extra expense of providing it.

"We have half-pigs in a red safety casing, since very often hotel and restaurant customers cart it off on a bike," says Tino Zeiske, the managing director of Metro in China, describing his company's attempts to ensure hygiene. "But buyers are equally willing to load an unpackaged pig carcass on a bicycle. The prevalent hygiene standard is, 'If you don't get sick, it's fine.'"

This sentiment is China's challenge, in a nutshell. It has produced a vicious cycle. The consumer has been burned by food scandals. The producers are reluctant to invest in building high-quality brands because they don't think the consumers will believe the brands are in fact high in quality. Everyone is stuck.

In truth, to expect transparency to lead to a quick fix to the problem is unreasonable. Transparency can be a great start—whether it's Wu Heng's website, Beingmate's advertising, or Metro's investments—but it is not enough. It takes time to get everyone on board to break the cycle. Consumers and industry alike need to join the movement over time—potentially an extremely long time. And entrepreneurs need to build a web of trust between producers and consumers, one that engages both parties repeatedly.

Indeed, a web of trust isn't woven in a short period—actually, it takes many years.

The Community-Based, Low-Tech Solution in Indian Dairy

High-tech may have the "cool factor," but sometimes lower-tech, community-based solutions get the job done every bit as well. In reality, there are many different ways to build a web of trust, and entrepreneurs need to find the path that works best for the situation at hand. Amul is one of India's iconic brands, certainly one synonymous with dairy in the country, and associated with quality, consistency, and affordability. Amul has woven a web of trust—enveloping everyone from the dairy farmer to the end consumer—bit by careful bit over seventy years, with nary a resort to punishment or threat of the sort favored by the Chinese state.[21] Amul represents a kinder, gentler solution to filling the trust vacuum.

• • •

Kanta *ben* ("sister") has tough hands. "My hands are so strong, if I hit a man, he'll collapse!" she says.* She holds them up for inspection. Then she demonstrates for her visitors how they got so powerful. She squats down under a cow and starts tugging at her bulging udder. She moves her leathery hands up and down, rhythmically squirting out small jets of milk with each tug.

She's been doing this task for ten cows, twice a day, for a decade. At this point it's painful for her, but she keeps going. After all, this simple motion has paid for the bounty all around her, and there's more to be done. As she milks, she talks about her chil-

---

* The names of the dairy farmers in this and subsequent sections describing Amul and have been altered to preserve their anonymity.

Lower-tech solutions: an Indian dairy.

dren in the United States. Two of them run motels in New Jersey. She visited another one in London for two months, but she didn't want to stay. "The kids were so busy it was boring," she says. "But when they come here, they work just like we do. That's what they grew up with."

Back then, her house was more modest. Now a quick glance around shows how far she and her family have come in the past fifteen years. They live in a *pukka* ("solid") brick house with a small courtyard. A Mahindra Scorpio SUV sits in the opposite corner from her cow shed, protected by a dust cover. A motorbike is parked next to it. Kanta estimates that she earns over six lakh rupees (about $9,000) each year, a very good living for this part of rural Gujarat, in western India. "I am happy," she says simply.

"She has been working outside for all these years," her brother Deven chimes in from nearby. "She started from one cow, and has become very successful. She's very healthy!" He ruefully observes that he, on the other hand, has worked in a shop or an office for the last thirty years. Thanks to this sedentary lifestyle, he developed heart disease and diabetes. "Now I am back on the land."

He, too, has a daughter in London and another in the United States. Over the course of the afternoon, Kanta and Deven explain to their visitors how everything—the house, the vehicles, the children's education and opportunities abroad, the overall contentment—was created by milk.

Indeed, one can see the results of this prosperity spilling beyond the walls enclosing Kanta's dusty acre. It's impossible to miss the difference between this swath of rural Gujarat and typical Indian villages. The buildings are tidier and more solid. The children are better nourished. Even the stray dogs seem healthier. The roads are in better shape and more of them are paved.

"Milk roads," the locals call them. The farmers of these small towns and villages have created this prosperity almost entirely by joining the Gujarat Cooperative Milk Marketing Federation, popularly known as Amul. These tales of success can be heard over and over again on visits to the dairy factories, headquarters, small farms, and village milk collection centers around Anand, the town where Amul was born some seventy years ago.

The story goes like this: A local farmer starts with one or two cows, bought with a loan secured simply by the fact that the farmer is a member of the Amul co-op (that credibility is all the collateral a bank needs). With that loan, the farmer is able to parlay his or her one-cow herd—through the sales of milk plus technical advice and other support from Amul—over a decade or so into a herd of, say, twenty cows. As the herd grows and the milk flows, the houses turn from mud to brick, the owner purchases a car, and the kids get a better education.

In rural Gujarat, Amul has effectively built a "development ladder" that farmers can climb to reach the middle class. While operations are still located mainly in Gujarat in western India, the brand now reaches far beyond that state: Amul is almost as ubiquitous in India as the cows and buffaloes that roam the streets and provide all the milk. In most Indian pantries one will find Amul: Amul *mithai mate* (condensed milk) for your tea, Amul butter for your bread, Amul ice cream as a treat for your kids. In surveys, Amul is perennially dubbed the most trusted food and beverage brand in India.

Amul grew out of a local dairy cooperative organized by activist farmers in 1946. These first members sought to break out of the exploitative system imposed by a cartel of middlemen, who took most of the profits from the sale of the milk. These farmers were advised and encouraged in their radical step by the famous freedom fighter Vallabhbhai Patel, better known as Sardar Patel, the "Iron Man of India," who struggled alongside Gandhi for India's independence from the British.

Then the farmers met young Verghese Kurien, freshly returned from studying at Michigan State University on a scholarship. Although he had studied nuclear physics and metallurgy, the government had sent him to learn scientific dairy management and had posted him to the backwater town of Anand as a dairy engineer.

Kurien was reluctant at first. Not only was he more interested in other, more glamorous engineering fields, he reportedly did not even like drinking milk. The fact that he was a Christian from Kerala state, and a bachelor and meat eater to boot, in a majority Hindu town of vegetarian teetotalers, did not help. The locals were so distrustful of this outsider that no one would rent him a room, so he stayed in a garage instead. Little did anyone know that he would soon stitch them all together in a vast enterprise, founded on creating trust across such boundaries.

Despite these early struggles, Kurien soon perceived an opportunity to lift the fortunes of these rural, impoverished farmers.

He started by fixing up some broken pasteurizing equipment that was sitting around the new cooperative's facility. Within a couple of years, he had become the general manager of the cooperative. He professionalized its management and began developing new value-added products while creating sales and distribution agreements in Bombay and beyond.

His success in Gujarat caught the attention of the central government. In 1964, it asked Kurien to replicate his model in other states. He accepted and went on to create India's National Dairy Development Board, launching many new dairy cooperatives in a program called Operation Flood. By 1998, after carefully nurturing and investing in the cooperative movement, this effort had transformed India into one of the world's biggest milk producers and Amul into one of the world's largest cooperatives and producers of branded milk. The growth has raised the economic prospects of millions of Indian farmers, not to mention improving the nutrition of entire generations of Indian citizens.

Kurien passed away some years ago, but his success is remembered as India's "White Revolution," a wordplay on the "Green Revolution" in the developing world since the 1930s. The name refers to the dramatic improvement in cultivated yields due to the adoption of genetically modified wheat and rice. This move likely saved India from famine in the 1960s.

How did Amul's revolution come about? The cooperative established a web of trust, relying on community-based solutions and patience to do so.

• • •

"We are built on the dual philosophy of 'value for many and value for money," explains R. S. Sodhi, the managing director of the Amul cooperative. "Value for many [refers to the goal of obtaining] the highest milk prices possible for our farmers, while value for money [aims] to provide consumers with the best quality products at the most reasonable prices."

Contrast the food quality problems in China with the guiding values that Sodhi says Kurien instilled in his managers from the outset: "Please consider your customer smarter than you. Don't think that you can tinker with the ingredients or weight. If you employ short-term marketing strategies, your customer will lose faith in you. We are growing, thanks to Amul's value system."

As Sodhi describes it, the cooperative's strength is derived from its involvement in and interaction with the entire process of producing milk, from gathering the original supply from the cows to selling the milk to the consumers. If both the farmers and consumers trust in the model, he says, then Amul has little to fear from the Nestlés of the world. Indeed, the likes of Nestlé have not shaken Amul's leadership.

Moreover, Amul's managers do not fear meddling from India's raucous political arena, either. Over the years, politicians have tried to turn Amul's farmers into "vote banks"—a group that can be relied on to vote for a certain political party. However, time and time again such efforts by politicians to co-opt the co-op, so to speak, to further their own ambitions have failed. "There is politics in any organization, but it is left at the door," another Amul executive once remarked. "The commercial cow is too big to mess with."

It is a big cow indeed. Although it does not process as much milk globally as Nestlé, the largest dairy company in the world,[22] Amul touches the lives of vastly more farmers: 3.6 million to Nestlé's 0.6 million in India. Amul is the biggest dairy cooperative in that country. Today, Amul makes more than seventy types of foods from milk collected from 18,600 village societies and sells these foods through 1 million different retailers in more than 4,000 towns and cities across India. Amul is firmly in control as the milk wends its way from the dairy farm to the processing center through the distribution centers, until it is sold to the final consumer. The group even has 8,500 franchise retail shops where only Amul products are sold, making it the largest retail chain in India as well.

What are the building blocks behind this success in building trust? And how does the community-based system work?

In Anand, the spiritual home of the Amul system, a now-famous "three-tiered" structure rules the day. The first tier is the village dairy cooperative society, composed of small household farms. These farmers join the co-op, paying a modest sum of 10 rupees for a share, and promise to sell all their surplus milk (beyond their own household consumption) to it. Together, these village societies comprise the eighteen district-level cooperative unions, the second tier, which operate plants that process the milk into various products and packages for distribution. These unions make their own decisions. They both cooperate and compete. The better-managed ones have expanded outside their territories of origin and across India, even competing in states where sister unions are based. And at the state level, there is a federation of the district unions, the third tier, governed by their elected chairmen.

Although cooperatives originating in myriad locations compete with each other, they also cooperate when they try to collectively push back against multinationals. It's reminiscent of Charles Shao in China, where Huaxia both cooperates by sharing knowledge with other dairies and competes vigorously with them in the market.

Amul and its associated cooperatives are all member-controlled. The farmers elect their own leaders—and those leaders return about 80 percent of the revenues to the farmer-member-owners. Compare that fact to the 35 percent share received by farmers in the United States and Europe.

Indeed, the web of trust envelops the community of farmers.

• • •

Still, while Amul's strength may stem from the building of trust through community rather than technology, like Charles Shao and Huaxia, Amul embraces the need to innovate. In the original dairy factory, the walls celebrate the visits of past presidents and prime ministers and, equally important, the evolution of dairy technology since the 1950s.

Here, the walls illustrate how Amul has leveraged various breakthroughs into greater efficiency and more value-added products. The co-op has used everything from refrigerated tanks to transport fresh milk, to something called a "continuous butter machine," a set of large stainless steel machines that process a constant flow of cream and spit out neatly packaged, chilled slabs of butter. When one enters the plant, staffed by workers in hairnets and run from a state-of-the-art central control room, the smell of raw milk is everywhere, but the milk itself is nowhere to be seen. Indeed, the milk is hidden in the gleaming automated equipment. Tetra Paks filled with milk and other milk-derived products stream steadily off gleaming production lines.

These technologies are important. While people generally consume the same amount of milk year-round, cows produce much more milk in the winter. What would the farmers do with the excess milk? Amul's plants convert this excess into dairy products with longer shelf lives to smooth out the swings in milk supply.

The guarantee that farmers can sell their milk, under any and all conditions, is the centerpiece of the trust that Amul inspires in its suppliers. For this pledge to be credible, Amul effectively had to *make* the market. But how?

• • •

In Isnav, Gujarat, about an hour down the highway from its first dairy factory, lies the beating heart of the huge organism known as Amul. The paths and streets are dusty and unpaved, but by the standards of rural India, it is clearly a prosperous community. The sun shines down on fields of grain beyond the *pukka* concrete houses. A couple of large tractors are parked by the road. In the middle of the village is a "square" of sorts, an open clearing with three brightly colored temples arrayed around it, each dedicated to a different Hindu deity. The square hums with activity. Adults zip around on motorbikes and kids run to and fro with milk containers.

Here, a line has formed in front of the Amul milk collection center, atop which stand images of Mahatma Gandhi and Sardar Patel, the latter being India's first deputy prime minister and a local hero. The farmers stand calmly in a line, waiting to deposit their milk in the tank (in crowded India, an orderly line such as this one is unusual).

The collection lasts about two hours, with a steady stream of villagers and milk passing through the system. The farmers bring the liquid in containers of all shapes and sizes, from a large cup filled by a single cow to a huge barrel. And they wait their turns patiently, without regard for social status, religion, or caste.

Indeed, these scenes are striking because of the tragic, generally tense nature of relations between often-in-conflict groups in India. For example, in 2002, just an hour's drive away from this peaceful milk line in the cities of Ahmedabad and Godhra, riots took place between Hindus and Muslims, resulting in carnage, disproportionately visited on the minority Muslim community.[23] But that violence was there, and this peaceful scene is here. Kurien had proudly noted in his autobiography how Amul had transformed the social structure in rural Gujarat. For example, women began earning as much as their husbands, gaining power in the household, since they managed the animals. A low-caste person could stand ahead of a high-caste Brahmin in the milk collection line, with no one objecting. Male, female, Hindu, Muslim, high caste, low caste—all were treated the same at Amul. And, just as powerfully, their milk is mixed together and sold as one product.[24]

The farmers themselves embraced this pragmatic approach. "This changes attitudes over time, completely," Kurien wrote. "The idea was to call this 'eco-social change' rather than 'socio-economic change,' putting the economics front and center and giving it priority over sectarian, politics, caste and other identity issues."

Community is important to build up trust over time. Technology is used in the service of building this community. For example, the collection is helped greatly by modern devices. Today, insulated and cooled in the tank, the milk can sit for hours during collection and stay fresh. Before the coolers were introduced, milk had to be quickly taken by trucks to the processing center to avoid spoilage.

Back to today's line, the process moves quickly. When a farmer reaches the counter, he or she is greeted by three co-op employees. One takes a sample of the milk and measures its fat content, getting an instantaneous reading with a little handheld device. Another records this reading in a spreadsheet. The third employee counts out the cash and hands it to the farmer, using a formula based on volume of milk deposited and fat content.

Around the corner from this stream of milk sellers is another stream, of people coming to *buy* milk. Most farmers keep some milk for their own household consumption (typically about half of the total) and sell the rest. Sometimes, however, when the cows do not produce enough milk, the members of Amul need to buy milk, as well.

Yet, something surprising is occurring. In one line, farmers are being paid about 40 rupees per liter for their milk. The next line over, their neighbors are paying 55 rupees to buy a liter of milk. This presents a riddle: Why don't farmers who have contracted to sell to Amul just sell directly to their neighbors? After all, based on what they are willing to pay, the farmers could get a price that's 38 percent higher! So why don't the farmers take advantage of this potential for arbitrage?

Pavan Singh is the deputy general manager of marketing at Amul, and a graduate of India's premier school of rural management, established by Amul in its vicinity. He explains it this way: "If they renege, they are out of the cooperative. If they are out of the cooperative, they lose their guaranteed demand. You see, the service that the cooperative provides is no-questions-asked. We will take your milk no matter what."

In contrast, if a farmer goes for the spot-price buy, she is trying luck from day to day. One day there might be little demand, and the milk will spoil. This dynamic is the cornerstone of Amul's model, the stable footing on which its "development ladder" is perched: Each individual dairy farmer, whether she owns one cow or a hundred, is *assured* a market for her milk. At all times, everywhere the co-op operates, the member can expect it to buy as much milk as she's willing to sell. And she is accordingly assured a return. Indeed, this practice creates a cycle of trust. The farmers have learned to trust Amul. The trust of the consumers is then anchored to their trust in the farmers. And so on.

Farming is an inherently risky way to earn a living. Farmers live at the mercy of the weather, not to mention fickle economic forces beyond their control. This certainty—this *trust*—is therefore worth a great deal to Amul's 3.6 million suppliers.

Just as significant, from the farmer's perspective, is the access that Amul provides to other facilities and services: counseling, insemination of cows, help with breeding, guidance on nutritious feed, veterinary services, and more.

This model is what granted such success for Kanta *ben*: a solidly middle-class life, a good house, children pursuing education, and lucrative careers looming abroad.

• • •

By contrast, a sixteen-year-old boy named Jignesh Patel demonstrates the promise of Amul for those just starting out.

At Patel's residence, an open courtyard is surrounded on three sides by a solid brick house. A car is parked just outside, inside high walls that protect the whole compound. The cows are tethered, feeding on straw on one side of the yard.

"We have three generations here," Jignesh relates. "Here is Grandma, here is Mama, here is the baby."

What does Jignesh want to do when he gets older? Would he grow his family's herd? Would he study in Gujarat and take up a profession? Start a business?

His two sisters have gone off to study in America. "I want to go to America, too," he says with a big smile. Other conversations confirm this sharp right angle in the Amul development ladder: Once people reach a certain rung, many want to head overseas. If he goes, young Jignesh Patel will join legions of Gujaratis who operate motels up and down the East Coast, or own and run newspaper kiosks in New York City. This path is common in this part of Amul's "milkshed." Farmers like Kanta *ben* climb up the Amul ladder, reaching a stable, modest form of prosperity—and then the next generation ventures abroad, to seek more opportunities elsewhere.

Another, lower-caste group will take their place on the ladder.

In this area, for example, the Patels are leaving, and the Thakurs are taking their place, the next stratum to rise. The villages become more prosperous than the average Indian village. But the general improvement and community investment hits a wall, because the milk money fuels the departure of the most entrepreneurial, talented people.

While Amul has cracked the issue of creating value and sharing it equitably—all along the chain from the dairy farmer to the end consumer of milk products—it has not yet figured out how to continually challenge the young folks working in the dairy industry. For them, dairy is not "cool," it is a stepping stone to a brighter future elsewhere. Nothing to sneeze at, of course!

But for Amul to advance even further—to transform its development ladder into a fast-moving escalator—why not imagine anew? Amul must imbibe the risk-taking ethos of the likes of Charles Shao in China, renew its openness to technology, and use it to captivate the younger generations benefiting from Anand's "milk roads" so that they not only do not decamp to New Jersey or similar locales, but also invest in their own local context.

That's its next challenge: to shift attitudes such that Jignesh Patel sees a brighter future right there in Anand—building his herd, studying, perhaps starting a new business that could benefit his neighbors—than he does in New Jersey motels or in New York City running newspaper kiosks.

• • •

Still, Amul has come a long way over the past seventy years. Previously, the milkman would deliver the milk. The milkman rode a rickety bicycle, wearing the same often-soiled outfit each day, the sides of his transport bulging with large and battered galvanized iron containers filled with milk. If it were a prosperous community, he might ride a Royal Enfield motorcycle instead.

It was common knowledge that these milkmen diluted the milk to make a few extra rupees.

Then Amul came along and changed everything. The cooperative built an iconic, hugely successful national brand that has fed hundreds of millions of Indians and offered many millions more a path out of poverty. Part of Amul's appeal, no doubt, is that it is a *desi* product—homegrown, something to be proud of (a mild form of dairy nationalism). But most of all, it was a product to be trusted.

This fact was true both for consumers *and* for the people who produced the milk. In fact, the cooperative model has this trust ingredient churned into it. Indeed, it built the infrastructure to make this trust happen. Amul exists to serve the farmer's interests, not to exploit her. "But," managing director R. S. Sodhi says with a laugh, "building value-added markets, building brands, takes a long, long time." Sodhi knows better than most: He's been with Amul for thirty-six years.

Verghese Kurien's farmer-owned empire was built on this trust, as well as some very shrewd branding and a judicious embrace of technology along the way. But could Amul be doing even more to leverage its proven model and the trust placed in it, to help more poor Indians climb into the middle class? Could the company place more confidence in its own farmers, trusting them to embrace innovative practices and new technologies? Of course it could. The next step is to build more of these "milk roads" out of poverty.

Reflections

In this tale of two entrepreneurs—Charles Shao's current endeavors and the late Verghese Kurien's past successes—it may seem that India's is the clear success story, built on the careful, patient cultivation of trust from both consumers and producers. And that China's example, by contrast, is a tragic, cautionary tale of the human and economic cost of a breakdown in societal trust.

Amul built up trust over many years, step by step. Rather than relying solely on technology to solve all problems, the group focused holistically on many different elements that produce trust (including technology). In doing so, it built a system that is strong and lasting and an iconic brand that changed the entire landscape of dairy in India. Although the beginnings of some success for Huaxia Dairy are apparent, clearly much more work is required before the Chinese dairy industry inspires the kind of trust that Amul has triggered in India.

So is China condemned to live with its broken food system, one in which the rich have options but the less well-off have to shrug, roll the dice, and buy the glowing pork?

Its problems are fiendishly tough to crack, yet this seemingly barren ground has indeed proved fertile for risk taking. In China, it is entirely possible that the next wave of entrepreneurs will leapfrog into a whole new realm of technology-enabled efficiency. The sole thing that's clear is that one-dimensional solutions—for example, Wu Heng's website—will not suffice. Systemwide change is needed. That will come from relentless experimentation, an understanding of the specific origins of mistrust in the Chinese food system, and, of course, plenty of time to sort out which experiments will have a truly lasting impact.

It falls to entrepreneurs like Shao, as the founder of an upstart, and Sodhi, at the helm of a revered incumbent, to weave and maintain the web of trust between consumers, producers, regulators, and the public at large.

They will take different paths to get there. Yet if these companies can figure out how to both *expand* the gains and *share* those gains properly, they might just usher in a new era—one in which everyone living in the world's two most populous nations can share in the benefits of a safe food system and in which the "ladder" to a middle-class existence gets extended upward.

Two

The Mindset Change

In the developing world, entrepreneurs must evolve their mindsets to look at problems as parts of an interconnected set that need to be addressed simultaneously. The entrepreneur rarely has the luxury of focusing only on a single aspect of a complex problem. Of course, this means that she faces a heavier burden than those in a more developed country setting. The story of a surgeon-entrepreneur, Dr. Devi Shetty, shows how this mindset change both elicits and contributes to the web of trust. Trust helps the entrepreneur create the conditions to create.

Reimagining Cardiac Care for the
Poor with Efficiency, Walmart Style

In Bangalore—India's Silicon Valley—Dr. Devi Shetty drives toward the hospital. Dressed in suspenders, a pressed dark suit, and gleaming shoes, he is coming from a breakfast meeting with a local politician. His Mercedes-Benz smooths an otherwise rough ride. A few minutes earlier, he had stopped en route to drop his daughter at school.[1] He changes out of his business attire into a medical gown as he speaks, his words interrupted by his clothes flying around the car. At a traffic light, there are curious glances from families precariously balanced on two-wheelers that pull up alongside. When the traffic can be persuaded to obey a red light, any traffic intersection in India is theater in action. Everyone is interested in everyone else.

Oblivious to all this, Dr. Shetty recites statistics from his crusade to his fellow passenger. "Do you know that less than 6 percent of those who need heart surgery in the world get it today?" His fingers jab in the air, the recitation of a practiced evangelist, but his animation and passion seem those of a young man—despite his being in his sixties. "And of those, two-thirds are in the United States. What happens to the rest? They die!"

Dr. Devi Shetty is the founder of the Narayana Heart Hospital, a premier heart hospital aiming to provide affordable, quality treatment for all those in need, regardless of ability to pay. Those who can pay more subsidize those who cannot—a significant mindset shift from the way most hospitals operate. The problem the hospital aims to solve is not merely how to provide top-quality heart healthcare in Bangalore. The hospital's solution takes other related problems into account—multifaceted issues that amount to increasing access to care—all in the service of lowering the cost of quality heart healthcare for the masses.

Indeed, Dr. Shetty aims to lower the cost for everyone, not only for the poor. Since the care at the hospital is so much cheaper than that of other private Indian hospitals, and produces better results, many ask why it doesn't charge more, so that greater numbers of poor people can be treated for free. To this question Dr. Shetty responds crisply, "Let's just be better, so that we can charge less to all, rich and poor." Questions of money in life-and-death issues are irredeemably complex; there is no way around it. For some, the charity that infuses the hospital is sullied by such questions. Dr. Shetty, the idealist, is also pragmatic. As efficient as the hospital is, curing the poor of the world will inevitably require raising money from outsiders. Enter Wall Street, suspenders and all, with its many complexities. Narayana is a publicly listed company on the Bombay Stock Exchange.

On this day, with an access road to the hospital all blocked up, Dr. Shetty and his visitor sit in a traffic jam on the highway. There are many ways to get to the hospital, but it's hard to know which works at any given hour. Someone in the hospital has been calling in to the driver, guiding the car rather like air traffic control. Dr. Shetty's visitor notes that this is akin to the circulatory system where different blood vessels compensate for each other and there is redundancy. But nature is more skilled than the public highway system. This analogy draws a bemused grin from Dr. Shetty.

This neighborhood chaos outside the car did not exist a few years ago. The land was empty, the hospital construction begun only in 2001. Every year, it seems as if a new level is added to the main heart hospital. Recently, newer hospitals within the Narayana group, several of them among the world's largest—for cancer care, for eye surgery, for orthopedics—are blossoming around what Dr. Shetty calls "Bangalore Health City." He triumphantly describes this Bangalore accomplishment as akin to what he witnessed at Walmart, in Bentonville, Arkansas, where he had watched in amazement as thousands of customers in their cars trooped in and out all day. Both his hospital and a Walmart supercenter have that immensity.

Ever the optimist, though, Dr. Shetty is neglecting one negative connotation of Walmart, the allegation that it underpays its employees and decimates local competitors. Dr. Shetty is referring to the positive aspects—the part of Walmart that excels at innovation and provides quality goods to its consumers at incredibly low prices. It is this version of Walmart from which he draws his inspiration.

It's an odd juxtaposition, healthcare and Walmart. But Dr. Shetty is methodically and practically preparing for the next steps to "Walmartize" healthcare. Just as consumers at Walmart can trust that they will find decent-quality goods at extremely low prices, so Dr. Shetty wants Narayana's patients of all incomes and social classes (including the poorest of the poor) to be able to trust that they can be cured, at minimal expense to themselves and to society. "Surgeons are revered when they restore health," he says, "but we have to be much more modest to improve further. Remember that the body heals, the surgeon doesn't. We just take the credit." It's time to reassess "normal."

To accomplish this goal, Dr. Shetty has not only had to look at the problem of heart healthcare slightly differently, he has also had to examine the problem as part of a much larger web of trust that needed to be woven. His patients needed to trust that they could receive quality care at an extremely low cost. His stakeholders had to trust that he could accomplish the mission of the hospital while still not losing money. His employees had to trust that they were part of something that could actually achieve these goals. Even when the infrastructure in the country did not seem to support this buildup of trust, Dr. Shetty and his team have chosen to find new ways to thwart tendencies to mistrust. The mindset change that Dr. Shetty underwent led him ultimately to solutions that, at their core, increased trust for everyone involved.

Imbibing Compassion, Mother Teresa Style

Dr. Shetty enters the hospital through the back door to bypass the crowds. Inside, there is the familiar face of Laxmi Mani, who joined the hospital early on, after she had a firsthand experience with Dr. Shetty's compassion and skill at treating someone in her family. She is the manager of the Charitable Wing, and Dr. Shetty

India: "A hospital built for the poor, but not a poor man's hospital."

later notes that she works for free. Laxmi is talking quietly to a distraught person who is obviously quite poor. India has nothing like universal healthcare or medical insurance, and this is a grand, modern, intimidating complex in which this person finds herself, in Dr. Shetty's words, "a hospital built for the poor, but not a poor man's hospital." The person Laxmi is counseling will pay what she can, or nothing at all, though this may not have sunk in yet. Laxmi greets Dr. Shetty as he walks by.

Laxmi Mani is responsible for quickly assessing how much each patient can pay. There is no infrastructure—in the hospital or in the country, really—to meaningfully and quickly assess this formally. In the West, in order to be eligible for subsidized care, the would-be patient would inevitably be "means-tested" to authenticate their claims about their assets and ability to pay, to determine how much aid they'd receive. The underlying infrastructure to pull this off does not exist in India, and when it does, it is still subject to some degree of potential fraud.

So Laxmi must use her intuition, and do so fast, to keep up with the flow of patients. She always looks each person in the eye, listens to their story, makes a decision and, incredibly, just moves on to the next patient. Those who do not need financial help, of course, bypass her entirely.

The willingness—and demonstrated ability—of the hospital to dispense charity just puts even more pressure on the doctors, surgeons, and the rest of the operating team to run a very tight ship. The more streamlined the hospital operations, including its surgical care, the less each patient's care costs the hospital. The more it can save from just over half of the patients who do pay something, the more there is available for the inevitable charity case.

Walking away from Laxmi, Dr. Shetty continues toward his office. As he proceeds through the lobby, he is accosted by patients hoping to get a word in edgewise. One patient falls to Dr. Shetty's feet, a gesture of respect in India reserved for the elderly, the holy, or, sometimes, the very accomplished. He stoops ever so gently to raise the older man and heads for the elevator to his office. Patients continue to recognize him, and, out of respect, withdraw from the elevator, as if to offer him distance. Their trust in him and the heart hospital is clear.

Finally, he reaches his office. In the back of his office are a shower, a bathroom, and a bunk bed. Always, there is the portrait of Mother Teresa, the Albanian nun famous for her charity. The portrait dominates the room, conveying patience, space, and serenity. Dr. Shetty volunteered at the Mother's *ashram* when he found himself running a hospital in Kolkata on his return from a career as a surgeon in London. Touched by her spirituality and selflessness, he was encouraged to think of ways of treating the world's children. So Mother Teresa is the other part of the Dr. Shetty model, along with Walmart. Curious bedfellows! And Dr. Shetty's hospital is profitable, to boot.

What kind of individual juxtaposes an icon of capitalism, Walmart, with the saintly figure of Mother Teresa, the self-sacrificing Albanian nun? This strange pairing in itself embodies Dr. Shetty's capacious conception of the healthcare institution he's building.

It might seem strange, but in fact these two influences, Walmart and Mother Teresa, may prove exactly the right combination to build trust, *create the conditions to create*, and provide excellent heart healthcare for the poor.

Interrelated Problems and Their Solution by Iteration

There are some fifty people in the antechamber leading to Dr. Shetty's office. They comprise about ten families of arriving patients who insisted on seeing him personally. No one is refused. They each are barely with him for a minute, moving in quick order through the spiritual chamber of the office. He is frequently interrupted by phone calls, with more coming in the weeks after he was recognized by the *Economist* as one of the most important innovators in the world in that year of my visit, 2011.[2] These calls, received matter-of-factly, seem uninteresting to him. Once, he refused to attend the elite World Economic Forum in Davos, Switzerland, to receive an award, since it clashed with surgery appointments.

Now that he is sitting in his office proper, the stream of visitors picks up. Student interns move in and out. Elderly patients touch Dr. Shetty's feet. Sometimes he appears to reciprocate, though he is usually, in fact, touching a patient's feet to check pulsations in the leg's arteries as part of his medical examination.

Around the world, heart disease is a leading cause of death. In India, the disease is one of the country's most prevalent.[3] Doctors recommend surgery for those whose condition cannot be adequately addressed solely with lifestyle changes.

For the most part, the surgical solutions can come in two forms. One of the most common is the coronary artery bypass graft (CABG). With this option, a vein or artery from elsewhere in the body is inserted in such a way as to serve as a different path for blood to flow, in order to avoid any blockages. The second option is balloon angioplasty, whereby a balloon catheter is placed near the blockage and inflated to create enough room for blood to flow. These interventions are both crucial and life-saving.

The problem is particularly pressing in India. As Dr. Shetty goes to survey the day's surgeries, followed by a phalanx of surgical residents struggling to keep pace, he notes: "Indian genes are three times more vulnerable to heart disease. The average age of heart attacks in the West, for instance, is sixty-five years, whereas in India, it is forty-five. When I was a student in London, it was normally a young son who brought his elderly father in for bypass surgery. In my practice in India, it is more often the elderly father who brings his son in."

Yet patients in India are inadequately served, since heart surgeons are few and far between and their services are mostly unaffordable to the masses. Most surgeries are performed in urban settings. Although approximately 2.4 million Indians required heart surgery annually when Dr. Shetty began his career, only 60,000 such surgeries were actually completed that year.

The problem wasn't simply about performing the heart surgeries themselves, in other words. It was about a greater interconnected web of issues, involving at least a lack of physical access to care, inadequate financing, undereducated patients, and an attitude of abject resignation to having poor health.

· · ·

On the heart hospital's third floor, two stories above his office, Dr. Shetty meets Dr. Colin John, whose productivity likely eclipses that of any pediatric cardiac surgeon in the world. Repetition is the key to productivity. Dr. John starts operating at 6:30 a.m. By the time Dr. Shetty does his first surgery, just before noon, Dr. John has completed three or four and is all but done for the day.

An adult heart and a child's normal heart, as Dr. John describes them, are essentially configured similarly. Adult cardiac disease often results from the clogging of vessels over time, rather than in any unusual configuration of the parts of the heart. In children, by contrast, the disease appears immediately in the form of strange architecture from the beginning, often triggered by a genetic abnormality. The heart organ might be backward or sideways. Indeed, the heart's parts might be laid out rather unusually, often in ways that can surprise the surgeon. There is much more room for major error and for unusual, unexpected occurrences. Experience therefore counts significantly.

Dr. Shetty and Dr. John are at work in different operating theaters in the same wing this morning. Between them is a third pediatric cardiac surgeon, a junior fellow who has trained in India and practiced in the Middle East. The rooms are brightly lit, with sunshine streaming into each operating theater. Music can be piped in, with some surgeons listening to Stravinsky, others to M. S. Subbalakshmi, the Indian classical vocalist whose Carnatic music is emblematic of the southern part of the country. Dr. Shetty has said, "Where is it written that we must have our operating theaters dark and forbidding, as you do in the West?" Whatever it takes to enhance productivity seems fair game.

The junior surgeon, deliberately situated in the theater so as to be flanked on either side by Drs. John and Shetty, can attract their attention easily through glass panes. This provides a sense of security for the younger man, as well as for the experienced

India: Sunshine streaming into an operating theater.

surgeons who worry about entrusting otherwise complex cases to newcomers.

This scenario is but one example of a concept formally known as "task shifting." The idea is that the hospital has identified tasks usually performed by expert surgeons that could be accomplished by more-junior surgeons under supervision. In turn, some tasks usually performed by junior surgeons are shifted down to lesser-trained personnel, and so on. The key is to ensure that, in shifting these tasks, the necessary safeguards and mechanisms are in place to keep everything safe and running smoothly. Not only is the junior surgeon's time less expensive, this also allows for each senior surgeon to oversee more total surgeries per day— often *many* times more surgeries than in the United States. More surgeries mean lower costs and quicker access for patients. Better yet, the situation actually provides a fertile training ground for all personnel, who are able to gain greater experience earlier in their careers.

This idea might seem small at first. But think about task shifting over thousands of surgeries in a year. Consider the algorithms needed to optimize which surgeon should perform which surgery, at what time and where. Ponder how to achieve all this without violating safety and efficacy concerns. One needs to innovate to develop the expertise to address this enormous complexity. Indeed, this is part of the hospital's intellectual property

Dr. Shetty's hospital has progressively refined these protocols and routines over the years. Its system not only assures the patients that they will have access to high-quality care but also reassures junior surgeons and other medical personnel and staff that they will be able to ask questions and have the opportunity to improve their skills. It thus cultivates and reinforces the trust in all parts of the system.

· · ·

A perfusionist named Vidya enters the room. His general role is to operate equipment like a heart-lung machine so that the surgeon can operate on a still heart. The less time the patient is on this machine, the better, to minimize heart muscle damage. At Narayana, Vidya's role differs from what it might be in the West. Eighty percent of so-called CABG surgeries in Bangalore are done on a beating heart, whereas the figure in a typical U.S. hospital is just 20 percent. Surgeons in Boston say that it is too risky to do most surgeries on a beating heart. Dr. Shetty's reply is that risk is in the hands of the surgeon. "When you have done as many surgeries as we have, you learn to control risk much better, you innovate, you use different materials, different tricks that work as well as the more expensive setup, if not better."

With task shifting, everyone has more responsibility, including Vidya. To handle that additional responsibility, the hospital must invest in significant training.

Vidya is completing his master's degree in perfusion at the hospital, part of Dr. Shetty's plan to train medical technicians who can help surgeons better leverage their time. His training will be much more comprehensive than that of a perfusionist in the West. Just like the layout of the hospital operating theaters has been rethought, hospital administrators have rethought which tasks must be done by surgeons and which by adequately trained personnel. This is important everywhere, but even more so in India and the developing world, considering their massive shortages in trained personnel.

Today, Vidya attends to a patient on ECMO (extracorporeal membrane oxygenation), explaining to a visitor that at the end of the day the heart is a pump and the lung is just a big membrane with oxygen flowing across it, depending on differences in pressure across the membrane. His job sounds a lot simpler than it is. A maze of equipment is used to keep the patient alive. The patient is in low cardiac output three days after a complex surgery, yet his heart is beginning to be brought back online. Aiding this is the ECMO and an intra-aortic balloon pump that can be calibrated so that, initially, the heart is asked to do only part of the work and so that the patient can be gradually weaned off his various machines.

The more responsibility that the hospital can grant to Vidya, the better. With this task shifting, patients trust that they will get quality care for more affordable costs, while junior staff can trust that they will receive a premier learning experience unlike that anywhere else in the world.

• • •

Similar to this task-shifting mindset, Dr. Shetty and his team have explored a number of ways to streamline, or, as they sometimes say, to "Walmartize," their tertiary healthcare system. He explains:

"While other hospitals may run two blood tests on a machine each day, we run 500 tests a day—so our unit cost for each test is lower. And this works with all our processes. Also, because of our volumes, we are able to negotiate better deals with our suppliers. Instead of buying expensive machines [like other hospitals do], we pay the supplier a monthly rent for parking their machines here—and then we pay them for reagents that we buy to run the machines . . . and they are willing to do this because our demand for the reagents is high enough to compensate them sufficiently."

The goal is to cut costs whenever possible while maintaining quality and trust in the system. The doctor who leads all of the heart hospital's administration offers even greater detail: "We don't sign long-term contracts. We negotiate every purchase because prices in India are very flexible and we don't want to be locked in to use a supplier who suddenly becomes expensive." To decrease costs and build trust, the hospital focused on lowering the number of administrative staff, to avoid greater opportunity for bribing found in other hospitals. Narayana even partnered with another hospital in the area to increase purchasing power and receive more discounts from suppliers.

In Mysore, a two-hour drive from Bangalore, a new low-cost tertiary care hospital is being constructed, with a design reimagined entirely anew. It is all on a single level, with entirely natural air- and water-cooled spaces, except for certain areas where refrigeration is needed, such as operating theaters and critical-care units. Natural materials are used wherever possible. Construction costs are miraculously lower by 80 percent than they are for conventional hospitals. Dr. Shetty estimates that he will be able to halve the already fabulously low cost per patient for cardiac surgery at his hospital over the next few years. Equally important, the single-floor natural structure blends beautifully into its surrounding village and is not alien to the hapless sick who live nearby.

Costs can be saved in endless and surprising ways if one develops the right orientation. Even fighting a tax proposed by the Indian government on all air-conditioned facilities might be an opportunity to ensure cost savings. The reasoning for the tax, no doubt, was that the rich have access to air conditioning, so taxing them is a way for a country like India to honor its socialist principles (the Indian Constitution, memorably, declares India to be a socialist republic). Unfortunately, and ironically, this means that all hospitals would be taxed further, thus putting healthcare further out of reach of the poor. Dr. Shetty has organized sit-ins all over the country to protest this tax, centered on the numerous facilities opened by Narayana Hospitals. "Ultimately, the tax was withdrawn completely," he proudly exclaims. "But I'd rather expend all that energy directed to sit-ins in taking care of the sick and the poor."

Solutions such as these—task shifting, cheaper supplies, innovative construction—do not mean lower quality. They simply mean more affordable care. Like Walmart, the care is reliably priced—and even reliably free, if needed—and the reliability and consistency is key to fostering trust. Without this mindset shift, it is difficult to imagine how more-affordable care would be possible.

• • •

At the entrance of the hospital stands a chapel. It is circular and divided equally into four quadrants. Each quadrant provides a space to pray in for each of the main religions of the patients at Narayana. Hindus, Muslims, Christians, and Sikhs all have their own place in this chapel. The quadrants meet at the center.

Remember Laxmi Mani? She is the sort of person whose office you visit when you need a good cheering up. Like a serene Buddha, her attitude reflects an internal calm. It is a curious happenstance that Mani's surname is pronounced "money" and that her first name is Laxmi, the name for the Hindu goddess of wealth. It is also serendipitous that her name aptly describes her work—for she is the person who dispenses money in the hospital. She is in her early fifties, with the slight creases around her eyes the signatures of a life spent smiling.

The entrance to her small office is on one end of Narayana's busy main lobby and waiting area. This morning, a line stretches from her door across the lobby; families wait with medical files and financial documents in hand. Almost half of all patients treated at Narayana will come into contact with Mani at some point during their stay—signaling her importance to the overall trust ambience at Narayana. For a patient, trusting that quality care can be found there is not the only problem at hand. Each patient needs to be able to trust that she will not be embarrassed or, worse, be turned away for lack of financial resources.

Laxmi Mani sits at the crossroads between Narayana's for-profit and charity work. For those who can pay, she determines how much they can pay. For those who can't, she determines how little they pay. How well she performs this task is critical to the hospital's ability to care for the poor. Most people do not expect to see a for-profit system so seamlessly juxtaposed with a not-for-profit one. But Narayana Hospital's administrators see the connections beyond what is conventional, further evidence of Dr. Shetty's entrepreneurial mindset shift to build trust.

· · ·

Several patients sit in a row of chairs pushed up against the wall, eagerly awaiting their turn to speak with Mani. This office arrangement is quite common at Narayana. The patient who is currently consulting with the doctor or staff member sits directly at the desk, while others wait their turns in the row of chairs behind. This reduces time needed to transition from one patient to the next. Privacy just has to take a back seat so that Mani can provide help to as many people as possible. Through all this, her calm demeanor helps make a possibly chaotic situation seem warm and comforting for patients.

The room is small, about 150 square feet, the desk littered with papers. Mani has been in this room, a glorified cubicle, five days a week, all day long, ever since the hospital opened. A fan whirrs in the background. A sheaf of papers makes a rustling sound but manages not to fly away. There is order in the room, but only just. It is a tight squeeze for those in the office, yet no tighter than in many parts of the lobby. Despite all, there is endless patience among those in the snaking line outside the door. In India, it is common to stand in a queue, a response to the shortages from decades of socialism.

A conversation ensues. Mani gently nods her head and makes consoling clucking sounds as a couple in obvious distress sits across from her. The man looks like he's in his late fifties, with the shriveled skin one sees on day laborers who have spent decades in the hot sun. In fact, he is just shy of forty. He alternates between staring at his bare feet, obviously uncomfortable sitting in Laxmi's chair—any chair. He blurts out staccato sentences, interrupted by his wife, who puts her hand on his thigh to calm him down, though she is beside herself, as well.

"Where will we get the money?" he asks. "We used up our savings to travel to the hospital!"

This patient is meant to pay $1,000 for his recommended procedure. But this is more than these folks could pull together if they saved all year, their daily collective wages being less than $5 (and surgeries can often cost much more than this $1,000 price). It is the kind of payment that would plunge them into endless debt. They are already apparently descending into that particular abyss. Most well-off Indians, if they are self-aware, will know of less-fortunate individuals in the penumbra of their own existences, who teeter continually on the verge of such financial mayhem. All it takes is a small, often curable, illness that removes the wage earner from work for a few days. The family must then borrow to compensate for the immediate loss of earnings, if only just to eat, and thus a vicious cycle ensues.

Laxmi Mani learns that the couple comes from the border between two states, Karnataka, where the hospital is located, and the one to the north, Maharashtra, home to the commercial capital, Mumbai. The respective languages of these states, Kannada and Marathi, are quite different. There is also Konkani, spoken in Goa, the once-Portuguese colony on the west coast of India, nestled between these two states. The couple seemed to be speaking a version of Konkani, incorporating some words from both Kannada and Marathi. Language in India, where the political boundaries of states were formed on linguistic lines, is a fraught affair; indeed, supporters of Konkani are often agitated at suggestions that it is derived from Marathi. To bridge the linguistic divide between the couple and Laxmi, vigorous hand gesticulations, a part of daily Indian life, advance the chatter and punctuate the background whirr of the busy fan.

An orderly enters, wearing a nondescript, clean but dull steel-gray uniform and a Nehru *topi*, a peaked cap named after India's first prime minister, who favored this headgear.

Laxmi grimaces at the report he hands her as he slips away. The report comes four times daily, detailing how many paying patients have registered at the hospital in the previous hours, and providing some information for her to calibrate her capacity to dispense charity.

The couple registers Laxmi's grimace. It prompts their own. Laxmi quickly rights her reaction and shifts from annoyance at the report that there were too few paying patients in the past few hours to the matronly reassurance and trust that she must convey. She turns back to the notes in the patient's files. Despite their visible distress, the surgery can wait a week while the hospital treats patients in her queue more urgently in need of medical help.

"Madam, we will not be able to wait," the man says. "We have no money. Can we stay in the hospital waiting room?" Although not medical, waiting there would create its own problems. One of the *sari*-clad workers assures her that a solution will be found. Laxmi says, "We will find someone who can help you find a place to stay."

This is quite likely. Laxmi maintains a list of local donors who give time, as well as small sums of money, to help. Indeed, among all her other duties, Laxmi looks for donors who can assist with the costs of the procedures for those who cannot pay. For this couple, some makeshift accommodations will be found to house them, more or less for free. But this will not address the couple's obligations in their village, of which Laxmi is unaware, and which no doubt animate their distress. As they leave the room, the woman says to her husband, as she is reminded of a more immediate need, "There is nothing to eat today." There are limits to what the hospital can do.

The interaction with the couple takes only twenty minutes, but to an unaccustomed observer it seems like an eternity. The emotional electricity in the air could be exhausting, but apparently not to Laxmi. She adjusts her *sari* and readies herself for the next situation. Like most middle-aged Indian women, she is dressed in this elegant garment that wraps around her body, with a portion draped over the shoulder. The *sari*—coming from the Sanskrit word for "strip of cloth"—has clothed Indian women for over two thousand years. Mani's is simple, but resplendent with color, multiple shades of deep blues and purples. She wears it in a style from central Karnataka state, where the garment around the midriff is pleated in the back rather than in the front.

When asked about the financing decisions Laxmi Mani has to make on the fly, Dr. Devi Shetty explains, "If we looked at the hospital balance sheet monthly, that would be like a postmortem report; the hospital would not survive. We have to look at it daily to adjust how we operate continually." In fact, all the key personnel, including the doctors, receive text messages multiple times daily, detailing the hospital's financial position. Everyone from the most successful cardiologist to the volunteer worker is converted, perforce, to a participating manager. In the United States, surgeons and the business of hospital accounting rarely mix—this daily routine would be considered a significant departure from the norm.

This integration of the financial with the medical signals the broader mindset change that is occurring at Narayana. The more that everyone knows, the more that everyone can participate in building the necessary trust to ensure that the system operates smoothly.

Beyond Bangalore's Boundaries

Sometimes, Narayana Hospital can do everything to provide high-quality, affordable heart healthcare, yet has to deal with the fact that patients struggle to even physically get to the hospital, especially so from afar. Often, even for these patients, Narayana is their only hope.

One of the best examples of Narayana's confronting head-on the problems caused by this kind of compromised infrastructure is its focus on telemedicine and transportation to its facilities. By tackling even these issues, the hospital signals to these patients that they are not forgotten—that they can trust Narayana. Telemedicine refers to the use of technology to provide access to healthcare in remote locations. It could be anything from a video-chat with a doctor in order to have a question answered to a more complete diagnosis from afar. Narayana has heavily focused on its abilities in these areas to provide care for those whom they may otherwise have been unable to reach.

In India, when patients cannot reach a cardiac care specialist, they often turn to their general practitioners, or GPs. One problem: The GPs have been known to prescribe the wrong treatment because they do not have the expertise or equipment to properly deal with the issue. As Dr. Shetty describes a situation: "If a patient with chest pains walks in to see a GP, the doctor usually thinks it is indigestion so he'll be given an antacid and sent home. . . . Twenty-four hours later, the heart fails and it may be too late."

The situation might seem dire, but Dr. Shetty was undeterred. He worked to establish nine coronary care units (CCUs) across India linked to either Narayana or another major hospital with the expertise, depending on location. Narayana outfitted the CCUs with all the proper equipment as well as video-conferencing capabilities and technical staff. Moreover, Narayana made sure to train the GPs to perform the proper tests. Scans would even be sent back to Narayana for readings by appropriate specialists, even when video-conferencing was not an option. The project had such transformative potential that the local governments got on board, offering to sponsor more CCUs. This is another manifestation of the mindset shift needed to address interrelated problems, in which Narayana treated the government as a partner rather than as a corrupt organization to shun.

Subsequently, a larger government organization joined the effort. Narayana partnered with the Indian Space Research Organization to ensure that satellite communication efforts would run smoothly. Without this outreach to the government, the telemedicine effort could not have been so successful. Throughout, Dr. Shetty stopped pillorying the government as corrupt, instead embracing it for what it was, while cultivating ways to nurture its trust.

Dr. Shetty conveyed how unbelievably beneficial it was to have such telemedicine capabilities available for patients: "If the patient does not require surgery, then the doctors may not need to touch him. . . . Once thousands of CCUs are networked, telemedicine can be self-sustaining for a few rupees per patient."

In other words, when the patients could not come to the hospital, or did not even know that they needed to do so, the hospital came to the patients.

Sometimes, this was literally so. Narayana set up buses to take specialists and equipment to rural areas on the weekends. On these visits, the specialists tested these rural patients for free, only recommending a visit to Narayana itself when a medical intervention was necessary.

• • •

But Narayana did not stop there. The outreach projects also turned global.

Egide and Alice are a brother and sister in their twenties, sitting in a whitewashed room at Narayana Hospital, talking on a cell phone with their parents in northern Rwanda.[4] Bangalore's afternoon sun is reassuring. Alice is recuperating after receiving a kidney transplant from Egide, her donor. Rwanda has only 0.2 physicians for 10,000 people, compared to 2.4 in East Africa, 5.6 in India, and 27 in the U.S.[5] Alice was informed by doctors in Kigali that there was no way to do a transplant there. Egide tells me only one such operation had ever been performed in Rwanda, by a foreign doctor, *"Mais, il est parti."* ("But, he left.") Alice doesn't speak much, though Egide is sufficiently recovered to do the talking, especially when he can speak in French. The siblings enunciate every consonant in their words, as is the case in their

Rwandan countryside homes, unlike the accent of Francophone cities.

It is amazing that these two siblings found their way to Bangalore. Egide explains, "I took Alice to the hospital in Butaro a year ago, after the community health center could not make her better." Butaro is on the northern edge of Rwanda, near the Ugandan border. It lies on a hopelessly bumpy road linking Kigali, the capital, with Goma, site of the genocide-prompted refugee crisis, just across the border into the Congo.[6] Rwanda and Uganda are troubled neighbors.[7] This doesn't stop Ugandans streaming across the border to the hospital that Egide mentions, created by the Rwandan government with help from Partners-in-Health, an outfit to which a famed Harvard physician, Paul Farmer, gave birth in Haiti many years ago.

But the Butaro hospital couldn't deal with Alice's deteriorating kidneys. Transplant options were also unavailable in the Ugandan and Kenyan capitals, Kampala and Nairobi. Egide is not sure how his doctor knew of Narayana, or indeed how he thought of India. It probably has to do with the decades of Indian professionals, including doctors, who have migrated to East Africa and maintain diasporic ties with India. Or with the fact that Narayana catalyzed a pan-African telemedicine network to link hospitals in Africa's capital cities with free diagnostic telemedicine in India, similar to its earlier attempts across the Middle East and Southeast Asia. Use of these facilities increased over time, nurturing awareness and trust at least in some pockets of urban Africa.

Telemedicine, however, doesn't come close to addressing Alice's kidney problems. There's the logistical issue of a cheap flight to Bangalore, involving multiple plane changes over forty-eight tortuous hours—an ordeal for the unwell. But without telemedicine and an attention to informational connectivity, Narayana's web of trust wouldn't transcend India's boundaries.

Back at the hospital, a busload of young Middle Eastern patients has just arrived outside its doors. They have been brought by an Iraqi, Ayad Abbas, whose family has a long tradition of philanthropy that predates even the regime of Saddam Hussein. Iraqi children injured in the various wars of the past decade used to be treated in the United Arab Emirates, though the price tag, covered by charitable donations, was some $20,000 per child. Abbas connected with Dr. Shetty—almost accidentally, through a yoga retreat—and Dr. Shetty offered to treat each child for whatever Abbas would pay. They settled on $2,000 per child, a price at which the hyper-efficient Dr. Shetty could easily break even, though others can't. Abbas said the mosque-chapel outside Narayana in Bangalore moved him. "I studied in an American Jesuit school in Baghdad, saying mass every day, and I am Muslim. So what? The chapel touches me. In the Koran, it is written that the Christian is welcome to pray in the mosque." Abbas remarks that there are certain charities in California that send children to Central America for medical help, but some are now rerouting many of their cases to Bangalore, given the compelling economics.

Even more than information and transportation, though, there's a prior barrier that often gets in the way of patients reaching Narayana. It's the patients' mindsets, much more than anything to do with the contents of their wallets.

Outside the hospital, as the Iraqi children stream in, curious onlookers stand on the other side of the street. They can blend into their surroundings; you have to spot them through the hurtling traffic and the animals. Typically, they sit on their haunches on the side of the street, oblivious to the noise, chewing *paan*, a mildly narcotic betel nut leaf, or tobacco. The street typically skirts what passes for a highway in India. The makeshift highway itself is used by bicycles and by heavily loaded bullock carts as well as camels festooned with finery and riders with resplendent turbans. Some of these onlookers are between jobs, looking for day labor; others are just resting; still others are clearly unwell, but they lack the confidence to approach the hospital. It is simply too modern-looking an edifice for them to contemplate asking permission to enter, even though they would be treated for free. They simply do not trust the system. Dr. Shetty knows that breaking through these barriers requires continual attention.

• • •

A surgeon named Julius Punnen, who was born in Saudi Arabia to Indian migrant parents, was ideally placed early on to help Dr. Shetty set up a cardiac unit in Dhahran in the hospital of his birth. Since then, he has taken on the role as ambassador-at-large for the hospital, in effect an emissary of the hospital's mission.

In Africa, Dr. Punnen explains, "There's plenty of advanced medical equipment—foundations and aid agencies donate this. It's just that after surgeons are trained to use it, they decamp to higher-paid positions in London or Toronto."

Various members of the medical and administrative staff meet to discuss current needs and strategy. Dr. Punnen marshals the views of those on the phone and around the table regarding what Narayana Hospital should do in Africa. There is a playful back-and-forth when someone asks, "Why don't we train 1,000 African physicians for free over the next two years? Maybe with a 'cohort' effect, some of them will stay in the continent rather than leave." Some respond that that would be too expensive, others that it will pay off with Narayana's reputation cemented in Africa, and yet others that it would be pointless. "If one trained physician leaves, so will a thousand," says one. Dr. Shetty, though, is willing to bet on the cohort effect and the ensuing camaraderie. It is easier to be a skilled physician in the company of peers, he states. Others say that the expense is beside the point; the intent is to serve the poor of the world, and the experiment is therefore worthwhile. A decision is made to initiate this ambitious training project with the respective governments. It is arrived at swiftly, some would say in a rather cavalier fashion. As the group views the situation, these continued attempts to solve seemingly impossible problems is better than doing nothing. It is also what earns Narayana its reputation as an entity to be trusted.

Reflections

Dr. Devi Shetty's entrepreneurial mindset has been central to shaping how Narayana Hospital continues to have a positive impact on healthcare for many poor people in its part of the world, and profitably. What is this mindset, exactly? It's that entrepreneurs should not wait for others to solve problems related to their own goals while focusing solely on their core mission. They don't have that luxury, if impact and scale are among those goals. In the developing world, problems come in packages. Each is part of a web of interconnected issues, so solutions to these must be imagined and tested simultaneously.

Coincidentally, Dr. Devi Shetty's work started in Kolkata, with Mother Teresa, not 150 miles away from Dhaka in Bangladesh, where Sir Fazle Abed's efforts to build BRAC predate Narayana's inception but continue strongly today. We encountered Abed earlier in this book's introduction. As with Dr. Shetty, Abed realized that to empower Bangladesh's poor, he could not focus on one problem at a time. Rather, he had to address a web of interconnected issues, all linked to poverty. A loan to a poor person does not help if there's no food in his stomach or if his kids are playing in unsanitary conditions . . . and so on. Both of these redoubtable entrepreneurs intuited the mindset shift toward *creating the conditions to create* by weaving a web of trust.

Three

Building on Existing Social Norms

Entrepreneurs will find it far easier to weave their webs of trust in the developing world if they capitalize on constructive, preexisting social norms and practices. These have often been in place for decades, if not centuries, in long-running, thriving societies. Here, we see this play out on a nationwide scale with entrepreneurs trying to develop financially and socially sustainable microfinance firms in both Mexico and India, while in the process propelling millions of their clients—mostly poor women—out of their subsistence existence.

Avoid Starting from Scratch

The little shop was buzzing with activity. Fifteen women stood arrayed in a U-shape, a ribbon stretched between them. Their songs and animated conversation bounced off the red-painted walls. Scissors were produced, the ribbon was cut, the women applauded.

The group had gathered at the Miscellanea Alex, a small, quiet grocery store in Chalco, a semiurban area that sprawls across an ancient lakebed on the outskirts of Mexico City. The name of the store seemed apt: Its shelves supported a sparse, miscellaneous inventory of cookies, candies, sodas, and soap. The corners were concrete pillars, the walls stacked concrete blocks. Next door, a pile of bricks sat next to a half-built wall—perhaps a sign that the owner had run out of money on her way to making the shop and was in need of a loan.

This moment may have signaled a new beginning, but the ceremony marked an end as well: Those present had completed a sixteen-week loan cycle with Banco Compartamos, Mexico and Latin America's largest microfinance institution.[1] As a group, their successful collective repayment of their loans qualified them for larger loans, presumably leading to bigger and better things. Thus, the celebratory air of a graduation.

This dynamic demonstrates "joint liability" in action. Indeed, almost all microfinance institutions start by using this approach: The women succeed and fail together (while men are sometimes the recipients of the loans in microfinance, women play that role far more frequently). For instance, peer pressure plays a key role here because each woman is accountable to all the others. If one woman begins to default on her loan, the rest of the women have an incentive to pressure her to pay. Otherwise, the group will have to cover for her, or forgo further access to credit.

The loan officer ensures that, if the recipient can't pay back the loan, the rest of the group ultimately does.

For the most part, the women manage the group largely by themselves, aided solely by the loan officer who, after all, is a stranger. The women only admit those they trust to their loan group. Others will not be able to join. This stability that the group provides is crucial for the success of any of the women's entrepreneurial pursuits. As much as we get excited about so-called "disruption," people really need a bedrock of stability to make any form of risk-taking work.

The microfinance institution thus builds on the social webs of trust already in place in the community. A conventional bank would not follow this approach; it would only make a loan if the recipient had collateral that could provide security, something material that the bank could repossess in event of a default. Yet these women typically don't have access to such collateral. Microfinance answers the call for a different solution.

The group members spanned a wide age range, from early twenties to late fifties. Many had young children on their hips. Two Compartamos loan officers stood in the center of the U and led the borrowers in a series of call-and-response chants to renew the women's sense of solidarity.

"Maria de Jesus, Maria Isabel . . ."

One by one, the names of the women were called out. At least ten of them had Maria in their names, testament to the deep affection and reverence for the Virgin Mary in this mostly Catholic country. Indeed, images of the Virgin Mary are everywhere one looks in Mexico, framed on the walls of dusty restaurants, ensconced in roadside shrines, sometimes even tattooed on people's skin. One famous image of Mary housed in a hilltop basilica outside of Mexico City—Our Lady of Guadalupe, dating back to 1531—is even credited with helping invent the very idea of Mexico, as an identity that fused that of the ancient Aztecs and arriviste Catholics.[2]

Many thousands make the annual pilgrimage on her feast day to the local basilica,[3] while others watch it broadcast on TV. Many Mexicans think of her as part of their family, their *madre*, who cares and looks out for them. Beyond merely sharing her name, these women likely also shared this cultural and spiritual inheritance, something that bound them further together. And, like their reverence for Mary, this coming together could signify something that ran much deeper than making a little more money from week to week.[4] Not that the money wasn't important to them. The women came forward one at a time to receive their promissory notes. They would later travel on a thirty-minute bus ride to the bank to hand in these documents and to have their loans paid out to them.

"How will you use your loans?" Susana, a manager from the main office, asked the *compañeras* ("comrades," as customers are called in the company's internal lingo, to signify something more than just friends).

One woman explained that she was planning to invest in her small grocery. Around the U-shaped gathering, one by one, the women named their businesses: a quesadilla stand, a small cosmetics business, a shoe store. "Buying textbooks," one woman said, a reminder that some who take out microloans use them not for a business, but for other investments, such as education. These entrepreneurs were pragmatists by necessity. They couldn't afford to be too wedded to one idea or approach: If cosmetics weren't selling, why not try tortillas?

The meeting drew to a close. Fourteen women had answered, but one remained silent. There was some irregularity in this woman's payment of her last loan, so she had been denied a new one. She looked embarrassed, but no one else made a fuss about it. Before leaving, Susana distributed little pink tote bags bearing the Compartamos logo—one with a school of bright pink fish swimming purposefully together in the same direction—to all the women. But she didn't have one for the woman who had been denied a loan.

It could have ended there, with a potential borrower cast outside the circle of trust. Walking outside to the minibus, waiting to ferry the Compartamos officers to another loan group meeting, there Susana found another pink bag. She ran back and gave it to the woman. It was perhaps a signal that, even though the woman had violated the terms of the contract and put the whole group at risk of being denied a new loan cycle, she was still considered part of this particular "family" of *compañeras*. She still merited their trust. And she would be given another chance to borrow.

· · ·

In this gathering of Marias who were clients of Banco Compartamos, the meeting was orchestrated to build on the social fabric already in place in their country. While loan officers are present and help direct the meetings, much of the experience is based on how the women interact with and support one another. Indeed, these women are themselves entrepreneurs similar to the founders of Compartamos. Just as with those founders, the women are building on their understanding of their surrounding society to weave a web of trust with which to pursue their endeavors.

Microfinance: Its Origins and Ubiquity

The shelves of Whole Foods Markets in the United States are groaning with "responsibly" sourced, local, artisanal, or otherwise premium products.[5] And, depending on the time of year, customers can even buy *Liberation Soup*.[6]

This product may sound hearty and nutritious, yet it isn't a meal—it's a cookbook. And its purpose isn't to make more money for the upmarket grocery chain, but rather to help Whole Foods give more money away. *Liberation Soup* is filled with traditional recipes provided by women from thirty-five countries, ranging from Vietnam to India to Nigeria, all of them recipients of microcredit. And microcredit, as one Whole Foods sign describes it, is how the company is purportedly "alleviating poverty worldwide through entrepreneurship." Of the cookbook's $19 price, $5 goes via its charitable arm, the Whole Planet Foundation, to institutions around the world that lend small amounts of money to poor people—mostly women—to help them start and grow small businesses.[7]

The Whole Planet Foundation presents a feel-good story for consumers. Anyone can donate year-round on the foundation's website or at the checkout counter during its annual three-month-long "Prosperity Campaign." The foundation then gives that money to partner microfinance institutions in as many as seventy countries, and those microfinance institutions (also known as MFIs) then lend the money onward to local entrepreneurs like Jacqueline, a Haitian running a shop that sells prepared foods and vegetables from her garden.[8]

Starting with a first loan of about $75—less than half of what an average American family spends on a week's groceries—Jacqueline has been able to expand her inventory and reinvest her profits into building a small sales kiosk in front of her house. She repays her loan in small installments, so the lender gets its money back with a reasonable rate of interest to cover its costs. The donor feels good. Everybody wins.

Almost every MFI has a page on its website full of photos of smiling micro-entrepreneurs like Jacqueline. Click and a micro-tale pops up, describing the entrepreneur's burdens, business, and size of the loan as well as what he or she plans to do with the loan. The story typically goes on to describe how the entrepreneur could bootstrap himself out of penury with some old-fashioned pluck and hard work, if only he had access to a small seed loan that conventional banks refuse to give people in such situations. These tales are so compelling that the promise of microcredit-as-a-poverty-solution has enthralled many development practitioners, philanthropists, academics, and economists for the past couple of decades.

The industrialized world takes for granted its easy access to community credit unions, to bank accounts and ATMs, to mortgages, business loans, car loans, and credit cards. But the world's poorest people lack that access. About 2.5 billion people live on less than $2 a day, and 2 billion of those currently lack access to basic financial services like loans and bank accounts.[9]

Conventional banks haven't reached them, for a variety of reasons. The banks don't have enough branch offices in rural areas. Or the sums involved are so small that the bankers don't think it's worth the trouble to make those loans. The biggest reason, though, is that the poor lack collateral. If someone defaults on a loan in the United States, the bank can usually seize a house or another asset to compensate for its loss. But the poor, by definition, have little or nothing to offer as security for a loan. Thus, their only option is borrowing from family and friends, or from predatory moneylenders who charge astronomically high rates of interest.

Over the past few decades, a host of unconventional "bankers" have stepped into this void, creating today's diverse "microfinance" industry, which seeks to go beyond loans to provide the poor with access to savings accounts, insurance, money transfers, and other services. Indeed, the rise of microfinance has been a race to expand financial inclusion to all—an effort that includes a diverse set of actors, from nonprofits to large for-profit institutions to philanthropic foundations and even to the World Bank.

Microcredit is actually older than even the two nonprofits often credited as its originators, Grameen Bank and BRAC, both of which originated in Bangladesh.[10] For example, in the 18th and early 19th centuries, the "Irish loan funds" made millions of loans to the poor, without collateral. Some trace their origin to Jonathan Swift, the author of *Gulliver's Travels*, who created a fund to lend to "poor industrious tradesmen" with similar checks and balances to those of modern microfinance institutions. In another example, in the 1850s, Friedrich Wilhelm Raiffeisen formed cooperative lending banks for rural German farmers that were effectively the earliest modern credit unions. This group model spread quickly throughout the world. Grameen and BRAC, two organizations rightly credited with popularizing modern-day microfinance, continued this tradition. Grameen would go on to share the 2006 Nobel Peace Prize with its founder, Professor Muhammad Yunus.[11] BRAC, described in the introduction, would eventually become the largest nongovernmental organization in the world, and arguably the most effective at reducing poverty.

So even though funds can be raised today with the ease of a mouse click, the animating premise of all these efforts has remained much the same. A group of people comes together to make a transaction fueled by trust and enabled by an appetite for a certain level of risk. Financial inclusion is being built atop a preexisting foundation of trust.

Microfinance has often been touted by well-meaning people as the solution to many problems. Yet, as with everything else, there are pros and cons. Yes, these services can create and expand possibilities for people living on the margins. But it is necessary to tease apart this hype from the reality behind the bold claims that microcredit would "put poverty in a museum," as a famous champion of the model once put it.[12] If only it were that simple! Indeed, done well, microfinance can benefit the poor greatly. On the other hand, the movement has learned some hard-won lessons about both the centrality and the fragility of trust.

Profits and Trust in Mexican Microfinance

Banco Compartamos was founded in 1990 as a nongovernmental microcredit organization that ran exclusively on grants.[13] In 2000, it became a for-profit corporation; two years later, it issued debt on Mexico's bond market. In 2006, it became a fully licensed bank.

Compartamos: Community-based microfinance in Mexico.

The following year it held an initial public offering.[14] Today, Banco Compartamos is a publicly traded company valued at $2.5 billion that serves over 2.7 million borrowers. At its IPO, it was the most profitable bank in Latin America.

This transformation has not been without controversy. Indeed, Banco Compartamos forced a conversation around the world about whether trust built on top of preexisting social structures can coexist with generous profits.

Compartamos operates unabashedly at the commercial end of the spectrum of approaches to microcredit. It generates huge returns for its private investors. At the same time, Compartamos has reached millions of poor Mexicans and has grown much faster than its nonprofit counterparts, such as Grameen Bank in Bangladesh. Therein lies the bone of contention. The name "Compartamos" means "let's share" in Spanish. Its many critics have

raised a fair question: Exactly how much "sharing" is Compartamos doing?

Michael Chu worked closely with Carlos Daniel and Carlos
Labarthe, the two founders of Compartamos (the "two Char-
lies," as they are known in the industry), in 1998 as they sought to
transition to for-profit status. He is unapologetic about the bank's
commercial success. It was, he explains, all part of their plan from
the very beginning.

Chu has played a significant role in the evolution of microfinance from a fringe idea to its current incarnation as an enormous global industry. His journey began as the former CEO of
ACCION International in the early 1990s, where he helped start
self-sustaining, commercially viable microfinance banks across
Latin America, from Peru to Bolivia. Chu explained that ACCION
had begun as a kind of "Peace Corps before there was a Peace
Corps." It brought young people to work in the poorest parts of
Latin America in the 1960s, building roads and clinics and community centers. But after a decade of this, in 1973 ACCION began
issuing microloans in Recife, Brazil, and soon was fully dedicated
to microfinance.

From the outset, Chu's objective was to make microfinance
a profitable concern—to build an industry where none actually
existed. "The whole theory of change was to show that banking
to the unbanked—financial inclusion—could be even better than
banking the [already] banked as a business," he says. "Because then
people would change their behavior and come into this industry."

Michael Chu describes how ACCION ended up in microfinance: "ACCION's people were getting a bit frustrated that they
would go build another community center or help a community
build another water pipe, and then nothing else happened. But
they noticed that every third door in these very poor areas was
a business—whether it was a mom-and-pop store or a carpentry

shop." Chu explains that these businesses had two options for financing: "Either the local moneylender, which is just anyone who has excess cash, or the last link of the distribution chain—the fellow who brings six one-liter bottles of cooking oil to the lady running the mom-and-pop shop. And she says, 'Gee, I don't have enough to pay you today.' And he says, 'No problem. Next time I come around, you pay me.'"

This pattern isn't so different from how struggling families in America financed their household consumption in the not-too-distant past. For example, in one movie called *The Prize Winner of Defiance, Ohio*, based on the true story of Evelyn Ryan, a mother in the 1950s supported her ten children and underachieving husband by winning advertising-jingle-writing contests for various brands. Before she started winning, though, when the milkman came by every day, Ryan had no money to pay. "No problem," he'd say. "I'll take your payment tomorrow." Essentially, he was extending her a loan.[15]

Chu's point is that plenty of people around the world are still financed in this way. But those means of accessing credit—through opportunistic moneylenders or suppliers' credit—tend to be exorbitantly expensive. "The poor were already paying the highest interest rates by far" in the economic system, he says.

Based on these insights, ACCION's mission evolved to extending access to lower-cost finance in Latin America, and Chu went on to help MFIs in ACCION's network transition from NGOs to licensed for-profit banks, such as BancoSol in Bolivia and MiBanco in Peru. But Compartamos was the first MFI to "go public"—that is, issue shares to the public in exchange for raising money from them in what is called an initial public offering (IPO)— to overcome the primary obstacle of access to capital. It leapt over that hurdle in dramatic fashion: The IPO was thirteen times oversubscribed. It was much more successful than even Chu had anticipated. He had thought Compartamos might one day be valued at $60 million. After the IPO, the value of Compartamos was a staggering $1.5 billion. ACCION and many other investors made a phenomenal profit.

Yet the juxtaposition of those handsome profits, with what some perceived as relatively high interest rates that Compartamos charges borrowers, put the bank in a difficult spotlight. Critics began to ask how well the bank was spreading the bounty of its efficient juggernaut of a lending system.

Perhaps the most vocal was Muhammad Yunus, the founder of Grameen. After Yunus and Grameen jointly won the Nobel Peace Prize in 2006, institutions ranging from the World Bank to the Gates Foundation had poured resources into expanding microcredit and researching its impact, as a promising tool in the effort to bring hundreds of millions of people in the developing world out of poverty.

But in the wake of the IPO, Yunus and others in the microfinance community became nervous about the "commercialization" of the sector. He argued that, by going after private finance, Banco Compartamos was abandoning its roots as an organization dedicated to helping the poor. It was in danger of becoming a glorified loan shark, he charged, levying high interest rates on poor women (most were women) and funneling the profits to fatten the bottom line of wealthy investors and private equity giants.[16]

Now, it's quite a stretch to accuse Compartamos executives, as Yunus has done, of becoming the "new usurers." Compartamos' annual interest rates, ranging from 65 percent to 100 percent (the rates have fallen over time), might sound terribly high to those living in the United States, but they're actually right in the middle of the range of loans available from both nonprofit and for-profit lenders in Mexico. For many Mexicans, the alternative to borrowing from Compartamos remains going to loan sharks and moneylenders who charge much, much higher interest rates. That's why Michael Chu believes that Yunus and other critics missed the point of what Compartamos and other commercial banks—and ACCION as an enabling institution of these MFIs—were trying to do.[17]

Here, Chu argues that keeping the interest rates high initially is part of the plan to eventually help more people and is, in fact, an important piece of the puzzle—a controversial claim. He maintains that when the first microfinance organizations in an area keep the interest rates high, other entrepreneurs and financial institutions will see the opportunity and be more likely to enter the new area as well. Further competition will create more options for the poor. Eventually, interest rates for all the microfinance offerings will be lowered as the various groups compete for more business. Chu argues that starting the interest rates high attracts more competitors, thereby helping more poor people in the aggregate than if he lowered the prices of the interest rates immediately on entering a new market.

"For [those who were nervous] it was very controversial, because it was a totally emotional reaction," he recalls. "But it's a red herring, this idea that there's a tradeoff between high social impact and profitability. If Compartamos dropped its price, for sure there would be 2.7 million families in Mexico that are happier. The discussion, though, is when you're looking at social impact, whether that's the relevant question. Because if you look at it systemically and you say there are 10 million families in Mexico that could benefit from microfinance, do you care about 2.7 million people being happier, or do you care about when the 7.5 million that have to be reached *will* be reached?"

He offers a stark metaphor: "It's exactly like saying you've received the distress signal from the *Titanic*. You turn your ship toward it, and you see the iceberg, and you see the *Titanic* going down. You see the heads bobbing in the water. You put down your lifeboat. The lifeboat picks up bobbing heads and then the rest of the argument is about what happens in that lifeboat. 'Would you like a second blanket?' 'Would you like coffee or would you like tea?' While the urgency is, 'How do I get other ships here so that they can start picking up bobbing heads?'"

So, the overwhelming media focus on the returns being generated for the bank's owners and investors ignores the view from those still bobbing in the cold waters—those millions of Mexican families that have no access to formal borrowing opportunities *at all*. Chu adds, "We've been discussing what happens in one lifeboat, and not how you make other boats come!"

Chu leans forward to emphasize this point. He moves fast and smiles easily, but he speaks in a measured, precise, reassuring manner that suggests he has considered what he's about to tell you from every angle and has already come to some firm conclusions.

Michael Chu is a truly global citizen. Born in southwest China, he grew up in Montevideo, Uruguay. After earning degrees from Dartmouth University and the Harvard Business School, he worked for a range of global financial institutions, from Kohlberg Kravis Roberts, the most profitable private equity firm in the world, to IGNIA Fund, a venture capital group that invests in companies serving the poor in Mexico.[18] With his wide-ranging experience, from the world of high finance to storefronts in the slums of Latin American megacities, he's developed a number of insights into our collective cultural hang-ups at the intersection of profit, commerce, altruism, and poverty.

"Instinctively, culturally, for many reasons," he observes, "we tend to associate high returns with greed, and we tend to associate service to the poor with sacrifice. And that's all about us; it's not about the poor. The poor, in terms of access to services, are just like any of us: What we want is the best possible stuff, at the lowest cost, so that whenever we need it we can get it, and we like to get it when we need it."

That includes metaphorical lifeboats. Chu wants as many boats as possible, as quickly as possible, to come to the rescue of the drowning poor.

At the end of the day, then, the question comes down to the following: Are Mexicans better off thanks to the efforts of Banco Compartamos? The answer to this question is a resounding *yes*. For many millions of households around the developing world, even in relatively more prosperous emerging market countries like Mexico (as opposed to less prosperous ones such as India), people's exclusion from the financial mainstream has dire consequences.

By contrast, in the case of Compartamos, perhaps another question ought to be raised, as well: Is enticing more boats to the scene of the crisis mutually exclusive with providing more blankets and hotter tea to the people *already* in the lifeboat? Why can't an organization do both?

"High return on equity is what will bring others, and the others will force the price to go down," Chu says, through the magic of competition. Indeed, in addition to the evidence of interest rates lowering in Mexico, this prediction is exactly what has happened in Bolivia, where BancoSol's interest rates have plummeted from 200 percent to 18 percent. In Peru, as well, Chu's theory has worked. More banks there have competed to lend to the low-income sector, which drove prices down.

Still, this pattern may not be the full story. It's a bit of a puzzle, especially when we take into consideration the results of a study done in 2013.[19] Two professors from Yale and Dartmouth, in cooperation with Compartamos, found in a careful assessment that cutting annual interest rates by 10 percentage points did not affect profits at all. But this move *did* substantially increase the volume of lending, putting more figurative bobbing heads in more lifeboats. Did Compartamos have to start with *such* high interest rates? Could it have lowered its interest rates a little and still attracted other competitors in the same way, while also earning a healthy return for its investors? This remains a contentious issue.

On the continuum of microfinance philosophies—with the aggressive commercial approach of Compartamos at one end, and the slow and steady nonprofit approach of Grameen at the other—where can the budding entrepreneur embarking on a new microfinance journey land? More important, which approach generates and nurtures more trust? Whatever the decision on this front, accusations of acting like "glorified moneylenders" do not help solve the problem. If anything, they probably scare off talent and creativity from tackling the challenge of how to reach those two billion heads still bobbing in the water. Individual entrepreneurs need to be aware of the ongoing debate to determine how they want to structure their efforts.

• • •

The Compartamos IPO planted a seed of doubt for some. Each new action by an organization either can add to the preexisting foundation of trust in society, making it stronger, or can deplete the trust, making it weaker. It can be a tricky environment for an entrepreneur in a developing country to navigate. Trust is something cultivated over time. Once built, the foundation on which it rests requires constant care and attention.

Nevertheless, no matter how it is cultivated or maintained, trust remains the oxygen of the ecosystem in which the entrepreneur works in emerging markets. Its presence, or lack thereof, is critical to the success or failure of an effort.

This may seem counterintuitive. Aren't markets, after all, founded on the idea that everyone is looking out for her own interest, maximizing her own profit-making opportunities? Which is to say, founded on *not* trusting other players to cut her any breaks?

Firms compete to offer the best services at the lowest cost, and customers choose accordingly. A healthy suspicion of "being sold a bill of goods" ensures that the customer gets a decent price, and value for her rupee or peso or dollar. So trust doesn't seem, at first blush, to be all that central to the operation of efficient markets. Why should microfinance be any different?

Adam Smith, in the 18th century, was right to marvel at the almost magical cumulative effect of each individual acting in his own self-interest. But he also emphasized that adequate levels of trust were a necessary precondition for the "invisible hand" to work its alchemy; without it, markets wouldn't function properly. For Smith, trust was the hidden engine of economic progress.[20] The borrowing groups were a potent example, a microcosm of this suspended disbelief that keeps the whole vast enterprise of buying and selling going, like so many dozens of plates spinning in the air.

The MFI model leverages an often-overlooked truth: that the lone entrepreneur exists in a web of relationships with his neighbors, with his creditors, his customers, his supplier, his bank, and so on. Indeed, trust allows transactions at all levels and scales of society to take place. With trust already ingrained in society, attempting to build that trust from scratch is unnecessary, and ultimately less effective. That trust already present in society is powerful—so, use it.

Toward this end, adding profit to the equation may not necessarily be the trust-killing idea that people sometimes assume it to be. Indeed, if an enterprise is financially viable and can use money to scale up its operations, then profit is the fuel that permits its sustenance and expansion.

My experience is that people have fairly fixed ideas on the extent to which it's appropriate to give profit a starring role in such settings. Some can't imagine not having it be the engine of dynamism. Others find it utterly opprobrious. Further, as a descriptive matter, my experience is that people rarely change their mind when presented with the opposing view. For the entrepreneur in question, therefore, it behooves her to determine where she stands on the issue, and to be aware of these often dramatically differing perspectives.

How (Not) to Squander Trust in Indian Microfinance

Similar to Compartamos, SKS Microfinance is a for-profit company that makes small loans to rural women across India. SKS is an acronym for *swayam krishi sangam*, which means "self-help group" in Sanskrit.

Down a dusty, rutted road outside Hyderabad, capital of the southern Indian state of Andhra Pradesh, a group of SKS microentrepreneurs were meeting.[21] Not unlike the Marias at Compartamos, some thirty women were seated beneath a spreading neem tree in a large circle. All were SKS clients, ranging in age from their early twenties to late fifties. They were there to attend a "center" meeting. In the SKS lingo, a "center" is a collection of four to ten borrowing groups of five women each.

It was the dry season, and dust from the hard ground blew everywhere, coating everything. Even so, a riot of color met the eye: bright green rice paddies and fields of yellow sunflowers, the women clad in saris of every hue and design. Children ran and danced around a circle.

SKS Microfinance: Women meet beneath a *neem* tree in Andhra Pradesh.

The "center" gathers each week at the same place and same time, and on time: Anyone who comes late must pay a 5 rupee fine, roughly 10 cents. The women repay their loans in weekly installments, ranging in total from about US$20 to US$250, and collectively figure out whether to disburse new loans. The women use these small loans for a variety of purposes: to buy fruit they can sell in roadside stalls, to buy buffaloes for milk, to buy seeds to plant in their fields.

The whole system was set up with the borrowers' needs in mind. The meetings usually happen in the morning, so as not to encroach on prime working hours during the day. And instead of spending precious time and scarce rupees traveling by foot or bus to a bank that might not even lend to them, SKS brought the apparatus of simple credit right to the heart of the village.

The only man in sight was the SKS representative. This *sangam* manager was the main point of contact with each center. (*Sangam* is a Sanskrit word meaning "coming together" or "joining.") He wore a simple cloth *jhola*, a shoulder bag much like the ones students might wear crossing the campuses of UC Berkeley or Wesleyan. It swelled with paperwork, forms, and ledger books for keeping the accounts. It also held some cash, but just a modest amount, to protect against the danger of loss or theft.

The man called the meeting to order, set his *jhola* on the ground, and removed some notebooks. Then he led the women in a recitation of a pledge, which functions as both a weekly renewal of their verbal contract with SKS and an explicit reminder of the commitment they have made to each other and to themselves, to use the loan for the betterment of their families. The small loans were useful, no doubt. But the ritualized repayment of the loan— which also enforced a kind of savings, really—was also building a larger resource for the women.

This call-and-response chanting, redolent of children's nursery rhymes, may initially seem corny and inappropriate for this group of tough-minded, hard-working adults. Yet rituals are valuable. They can encourage the formation of good habits and cement a sense of community, merely by articulating a few basic principles and explicit intentions out loud on a regular basis, in a kind of public theater.

For example, one distinctive thing about those pledges is the tense: The women were focusing on the future. "I *will* repay my loan on time . . . I *will* help my neighbor. . . ." These weren't just words, but public commitments to future actions. The women were making plans, cementing the habit of *aspiring*.

The anthropologist Arjun Appadurai has described the important and overlooked need to help the poor build their "capacity to aspire."[22] The poor, he reminds us, have fewer opportunities than do rich people to imagine better futures, as well as a narrower range of experiences to draw on. In this sense, the larger value of the SKS center and its subgroups is that they provide a constructive forum within which women aspire together.

The brief ritual concluded, the *sangam* manager announced the main order of business: the weekly repayment of their loans. The leaders of each five-woman borrowing group came up, one by one, and handed a stack of rumpled rupee notes to the *sangam* manager. He counted it and entered the amount into their passbooks, laid out for anyone to see. The modest sums reflected the cash flow of their micro-enterprises, which can fluctuate from week to week. Then he discussed new loan applications with the leaders of each borrowing group. The women recited the pledge again, and the meeting was over.

Within the group, two women clearly were in charge of ensuring repayment and inspiring confidence in the others. They were the shepherds, in effect, who exerted gentle pressure to maintain discipline and to resist the temptation to spend precious rupees on consumption instead of on their enterprises.

As the women dispersed, just across the dusty patch of ground, another conversation was unfolding in a small group of women. They were discussing two other members of the center, who had already departed for the fields.

"They should not get another loan!" one woman was saying with vehemence.

"But they have paid back every week," another replied, "just like we have."

"They both have taken other loans—and from moneylenders."

"They owe too much money!"

"She cannot earn enough from her shop to pay back all those loans."

"If they cannot pay, we will have to pay for them."

The debate was fairly animated. Apparently, the absent women were in some kind of gray area: They hadn't missed a single repayment, but their peers weren't confident of their ongoing ability to sustain their payments. They had taken out loans from two or three other MFIs—all engaged in the rough-and-tumble competition to make loans—and one had borrowed from a local moneylender who showed up regularly, aggressively demanding repayment. These new loans had been taken out to repay the original loans, and the women in the debate feared the consequences of their peers' continuing to borrow from one entity to repay another. It was only a matter of time before this overborrowing would catch up with them, and the other women in the subgroup knew it. And they certainly didn't want to bear the cost of their neighbors' recklessness. Just like the women in Compartamos, these women were demonstrating the effects of joint liability in action.

It wasn't enough for the borrowers to exercise discipline on their own. A vast body of social science has confirmed that individuals succumb to temptation. The peer pressure exerted by the group members on each other was one force strong enough to ensure that each member would repay. The genius of this practice is that it outsources the resolution of the age-old problem of "moral hazard"—someone taking an ill-advised risk because its consequences will be borne by others—to the community itself, by using the existing kinship and other social networks as scaffolding to build trust and discipline within the borrowing group. And while it produces some stresses, such as the disagreement between the women of that SKS group, these generally pale in comparison to the stress of paying an exorbitant 200 percent interest to a moneylender. Thus, the trust is built on top of the social structures already in place.

Meanwhile, the *sangam* manager was busy answering questions from another group of women. It was part of his job to keep his ear to the ground, to stay attuned to the group dynamics. He came from this part of Andhra Pradesh, spoke the same dialect as the women, and understood their culture, since it was also *his* culture. But SKS rules precluded staff from managing centers in their own villages, to avoid any possibility of corruption. This arrangement came with a tradeoff: Although someone from this community would have a better sense of the group dynamics, they might be more susceptible to local social pressures, which could compromise the fairness and transparency of the lending and repayment processes. Counterintuitively, the outsider would inspire *more* trust.

The *sangam* manager got ready to depart for his next center meeting. In a typical week, he might run four of these meetings each morning, traversing the countryside on motorbikes and buses to reach each of the twenty center groups he supervises. Then he'd head back to the branch office, where he would spend a few tedious hours entering all the data gathered that day into the computer and preparing to follow the same routine the next day.

Efficiency—evident in the brisk, businesslike way the center meeting was conducted, and in the tight schedule kept by each *sangam* manager—was central to the SKS model. It largely explained how SKS has grown much faster than other microfinance institutions in India. But the nation's poor roads, combined with the fact that most of its unbanked citizens live in rural villages far from any branch office, still posed some daunting logistical challenges for SKS *sangam* managers—and for the executives in Hyderabad.

Technology offered a potential way around this bottleneck. At the time, cheap smartphones weren't widely available, and mobile phones weren't yet ubiquitous, though the trends were clear:

Mobile phone subscriber numbers were climbing rapidly. During this period of growth for SKS, the board speculated that if it could harness the huge potential that mobile technology offered to leapfrog over the hurdles of India's woeful infrastructure, SKS could become a truly transformative institution for India's poor.

As it turned out, though, technology is merely a sideshow in comparison to the key factor: trust.

• • •

In 2010, SKS was slated to go public on the Bombay Stock Exchange. Much like the Compartamos IPO before it, the SKS offering was generating soul-searching in the broader development and microfinance communities. Even though SKS charged much lower interest rates to its clients than did Compartamos, the angst levels seemed every bit as high. A question was being murmured at conferences and occasionally shouted on the opinion pages of big newspapers: Could investors who primarily sought financial gain, rather than social impact, be *trusted* to drive the microfinance vehicle?

SKS executives replied to such arguments by pointing out that the only way to grow fast enough to reach India's 450 million unbanked people was to bring in private finance. India's government is renewing efforts to extend banking services to the rural poor, in its own lumbering way, yet for many people the only option in emergencies is still turning to predatory moneylenders for loans.

Grameen Bank, the microfinance institution that captured the modern imagination, had wrought wonders, reaching some seven million Bangladeshi households. But it took decades to do it by operating in a manner quite distinct from that of a for-profit company.[23] With Grameen's approach, it would take a colossal amount of time to make a dent in India's problem of financial inclusion. Indeed, Grameen's approach had come with an implicit social cost—slow rollout of loans. SKS could explore solving this problem much more quickly with a for-profit model while still remaining equally concerned with keeping interest rates low.

Still, against this backdrop, the IPOs of Compartamos in 2007 and of SKS in 2010 had given the media a nicely Manichaean puzzle to play with: Was microcredit still about altruism and helping people overcome poverty, or was it now just another way to make money off the poor? And can society trust such a group?

Those are some strong cultural headwinds for any entrepreneur ready to take a risk and start a new endeavor.

• • •

Three months after SKS launched its IPO, in October 2010, the company was perhaps India's fastest-growing financial institution—and suddenly one of its most controversial.

In late July, SKS Microfinance's IPO had broken records, raising $350 million from a range of investors—one of the most successful listings in twenty-five years in India. The total value of the company's shares of stock went to $2 billion almost overnight, an unprecedented event for a company focused squarely on the poor, anywhere in the world.

But suddenly the SKS stock price dropped like a stone.

It lost 96 percent of its value in the space of a few days. Something was seriously wrong.

Every MFI operating in Andhra Pradesh, SKS included, was being accused of *exploiting* the poor. The newspapers were publishing lurid accusations against loan officers from many MFIs, claiming they were pushing desperate clients who had overborrowed and failed to repay to the brink of suicide, through coercion, public shaming, and other aggressive tactics. Seventeen SKS staff—and many from other organizations as well—had been jailed.

All the hard-fought gains dating from the company's inception as a small nonprofit in 1997 were at risk. The whole industry seemed on the verge of collapse, and the microcredit model itself seemed at risk of being discredited. The consequence would be millions of poor Indians losing their only alternative to greedy loan sharks for accessing credit—all this turmoil arising from the simple loss of trust in these organizations.

How on earth had this happened?

On October 15, 2010, the state government issued an executive order that restricted lending by all MFIs operating in the state,[24] requiring them to go through local government channels to collect loan repayments, and to get prior approval for each new loan. This move would raise the cost of administering each loan so substantially that it would effectively destroy the efficiency that enabled low-cost finance for the poor.

Indeed, that was its goal. *The Economist* magazine correctly identified the central causal factor right in the midst of the crisis: "The growth of microfinance has reduced local politicians' ability to use rural credit as a tool of patronage. That puts MFIs in the firing line."

Witnessing the rapid growth of the professionally managed MFIs, greedy local players felt that they were getting elbowed aside in a new gold rush. The government-funded "self-help groups" charged nominally lower interest rates on their loans, but the delivery of the money and the repayment of dues were cumbersome and fraught with corrupt practices. As a result, most women preferred the reliability of organized loans, cleanly and efficiently delivered by private sector MFIs, even though the rates were nominally higher than ostensibly "almost-free" government-delivered credit.

In short, the SKS loan experience was vastly better, so the government's self-help groups were rapidly losing their customer base. Middlemen could no longer siphon off nearly as much money from the government's program. They faced an existential threat. So, they responded accordingly, manipulating the levers of state government to protect their racket. Like a frustrated board game player falling further and further behind, they decided to upend the entire playing board rather than continue playing.

The ordinance went even further: Local officials were also given the power to unilaterally and arbitrarily revoke loan registrations—exactly what poor women tried to avoid at the hands of government loan officers before the advent of the professionalized industry. The immediate effect of these onerous requirements was to shut down new lending, and to signal to borrowers that they need not repay their loans. Indeed, the women stopped repaying their loans because they did not think they would be able to access loans from professional firms in the future, as they would have otherwise. Why bother paying? Although it was promoted by its authors as "an ordinance to protect the women Self-Help Groups from exploitation by the Micro Finance Institution," sadly, it would instead wind up victimizing those women first and foremost.

On October 22, the SKS board gathered to address the crisis. The meeting would normally have taken place at the SKS head office in the Kundanbagh Colony area of Hyderabad, but as a precaution it was shifted to a conference room at the Novotel Hotel (with easy access to the airport).

The location was kept confidential. That same day, police had arrested even more loan officers from SKS and another MFI. The situation was fluid and chaotic enough that there were fears that the police might come and detain management, too—they had already talked openly of arresting Vikram Akula, the charismatic founder of SKS. India is far from a lawless country, but the wheels of justice there grind slowly and often imperfectly.

The arrested SKS employees were booked under a grab-bag of charges, as though their jailers had flipped through the Indian penal code and selected at random: section 384, extortion; section 506, intimidation; section 448, house trespassing; and section 109, abetting the crime of another. Many were also charged under section 306: "abetting suicide." Outrageous accounts circulated in the local media of mafia-like tactics to collect on debts, claiming that loan officers from various MFIs encouraged borrowers who couldn't pay back multiple loans to take their own lives. Any kind of intimidation or aggressive behavior was, of course, completely forbidden by both SKS policy and company culture, and almost all the detained men had worked with SKS for several years.

The loan officers all came from the same impoverished villages as the borrowers. Some were taken from their homes in the middle of the night, terrifying their wives and children. One man, Mahender, spent twenty-seven days in jail, in the same cell as people accused of armed robbery and murder. Soon after he was taken into custody, his pregnant wife took ill and they lost the child. Another staff member, Sambasiva Rao, spent twenty-four days in a central jail, where the authorities didn't give him access to adequate food and clothing for the first week. Most of the detained men reported that the police were verbally abusive. The police didn't let them post bail, so they languished in jail, uncertain about their families, their futures, and their reputations in their communities.

It's likely that local moneylenders and loan sharks of some MFIs *did* engage in some of these coercive abusive tactics. Yet the media incorrectly lumped all the nongovernment lenders operating in Andhra Pradesh into one big villain.

Throughout these few weeks, K.V. Rao, the head of SKS's operations, kept close tabs on his employees' status and welfare. Many nights he was up until 1 a.m. making phone calls, trying to track down and inform their families, and talking with other officials. SKS lined up legal counsel for the men and paid all legal expenses. Without bribing anyone, they managed to persuade the police to stop ill-treating the detainees, and to let SKS provide food and clothing for the men in jail. He also reassured other SKS loan officers, who were wondering whether they would lose their jobs due to the restricted lending.

And meanwhile, to understand exactly what was happening on the ground, he reached out to the purported accusers. Those clients all told him the same thing.

"They clearly said, 'How can this boy be responsible for what happened to our family? We borrowed, and we got pressure from the collection tactics of other lenders, not SKS,'" Rao recalls. These clients gave statements to the courts and police, exonerating the loan officers.

A report by the Andhra Pradesh Society for Elimination of Rural Poverty later found that fifty-four people who were microfinance borrowers committed suicide, perhaps partly due to harassment from loan officers. Data from SERP and from the National Crime Records Bureau suggest that the overall suicide rate among MFI borrowers in Andhra Pradesh is actually lower than the state-wide average, which nevertheless is tragically high, at over 16 per 100,000 citizens. None of those who committed suicide were actually in default on loans from SKS, rendering dubious any claims of direct causation by loan officer misbehavior.

In other words, state officials cynically turned these private tragedies into a rationale for protecting their state-run, self-help lending scheme. The resulting damage was mostly inflicted on their own poor constituents.

Many clients said they were pressured by village leaders to speak out against SKS and other MFIs. The access of these clients to government welfare programs (such as subsidized cooking gas and seeds) had been used as leverage. Politicians, media talking heads, and analysts who had never set foot in Andhra Pradesh were all weighing in, claiming loudly and stridently to speak on behalf of the poor.

In the thick of the crisis, the company's leaders had to focus on multiple fronts. Since SKS was now a publicly traded company, it had a fiduciary responsibility to its shareholders, especially as the stock price was starting to fall precipitously. It had a moral responsibility to protect and support its staff. And it had a legal and moral responsibility to protect the firm's short- and long-term ability to serve India's financially excluded poor. This, after all, was the company's mission.

The web of trust that had supported the whole enterprise was unraveling in Andhra Pradesh, even as the board met. The uncertainty conjured by the new ordinance made borrowers wonder if they should even keep coming to weekly meetings. And if all the lenders were going under, another key motivation to repay one's loan—the prospect of getting a new loan in the future—was removed, too. The fear was that borrowers would cease repaying loans because they were being told—by the media, by self-serving politicians, by competitors—that SKS wouldn't be around to collect for much longer, so "don't throw your money down the drain."

As the board met in the midst of this furor, it discussed worst-case scenarios and how to brace SKS for them. What if SKS and other MFIs operating in Andhra Pradesh weren't able to repay their *own* loans from conventional banks? This issue was critical to the continued existence of the organization. Unlike MFIs elsewhere, SKS was funded by borrowings from banks and the capital market rather than by deposits. The ability to pay back these loans relied heavily on Andhra Pradesh. After all, 30 percent of SKS's loan portfolio was in that Indian state. And, of course, it would be much worse if the toxic suspicions spread to India's other states.

If a loss of trust is what led to the MFI crisis in the first place, then maintaining and rebuilding trust would be key as SKS worked to move forward.

• • •

Within a few weeks, the seventeen staff members were released without charges. Later, they would be fully exonerated. (Some still work for SKS today; the rest were let go or resigned because the crisis shrank SKS operations in Andhra Pradesh dramatically.)

It became clear that SKS management would need to keep its head down, let the storm pass, and stick to the high road. It could have pursued cases against the agitators and abusive police, but it chose to look to the bigger challenges on the horizon.

In the period that followed this series of events, the fallout played out in the media, the courts, and the credit markets. Experts wrote op-ed pieces in major newspapers laying the blame, much like the *Economist* did, at the door of the government self-help group bureaucrats.[25] Still, the views of distant academics wouldn't have much influence on the short-run outcome.

The leaders of SKS were in a battle, rather, with rumormongers in the local Telugu-language press. In this respect, the crisis was very different from the backlash in the wake of the Compartamos IPO in Mexico, which played out almost entirely on globally read op-ed pages and in academic confabs.

"If some academic in Hong Kong had said something, it wouldn't have affected us," says SKS's then-chief financial officer, Dilli Raj. "But this backlash took place on our home ground."

Tip O'Neill, the talented Boston politician in the 1970s and a former Speaker of the U.S. House of Representatives, once said that "all politics is local." This statement was as true of Andhra

Pradesh in 2010 as it was of the Boston of that era. Some in the lo-cal media were connected to the political actors behind the crisis. Their coverage only inflamed the situation. Certain press outlets may have had good intentions, but had a hard time separating rumor from the facts on the ground.

In sum, there was plenty of *mis*trust to go around. As it turns out, creating mistrust is easier than creating trust.

In late 2010 and early 2011, SKS leaders had to navigate careful-ly, trying to quietly restore the faith of regulators and the banks. The central government's rules require lenders to lend to disad-vantaged people, especially in rural parts of India. MFI loans were counted in that category, so banks had an incentive to lend to SKS and others, so that they in turn could lend to the poor and so that the conventional banks could meet their legal requirements.

With the advent of the crisis, the government changed its tune, signaling it might no longer want to support this arrangement. The banks then became skittish. Dilli Raj was emphatic, vowing: "We can't *not* pay the banks." If SKS violated the terms of its loans, the banks wouldn't be allowed to lend to SKS again. More-over, SKS needed to maintain the trust of the banks. That trust was an "asset" of utmost importance.

Quietly, SKS executives went into overdrive, spreading the mes-sage of taking the high road, explaining what happened, prepar-ing the ground to rebuild trust. They rationalized the SKS struc-ture. Some branches were cut out and streamlined, and more risk metrics were put in place, ensuring that SKS wasn't overexposed to the political vagaries of any one particular state. SKS largely wrote off the losses in Andhra Pradesh, and set about raising pri-vate capital again once the market had settled down. SKS was the only big MFI to honor all its commitments to the conventional banks. So it avoided bankruptcy, and emerged from the wreckage intact, largely due to a focus on rebuilding trust. Several other microfinance lenders did not fare as well. They went bankrupt. The central bank, the economic advisors to the government, the Supreme Court—all eventually came to fair-minded, evenhanded conclusions about the causes of the crisis and who was to blame. But this denouement would take about three years. Five years later, a Supreme Court ruling cleared all the MFIs of wrongdoing.

CEO M. R. Rao reflected, "The customers still trust us. But [our success is] nothing to write home about," because the poor of Andhra Pradesh didn't fare as well. SKS and other MFIs stopped lending in the state. Two years after the crisis, a survey found that most people were borrowing again from pawnbrokers, farm product intermediaries, and moneylenders. Some charged interest rates of as great as 225 percent. Moreover, even though the professed level of trust from customers for SKS is exceedingly high, SKS cannot trust the Andhra Pradesh state-level machinery from descending into chaos again, and so has had to stay entirely away. To rebuild SKS Microfinance, the organization would have to rely on other regions outside of Andhra Pradesh.

• • •

In evaluating this crisis, it is clear that the ultimate cause was a severe and sudden loss of trust from the community in which organized microfinance firms operated. Remember, the rule is to build with what you already have. SKS's plummeting stock price was a signal of local society's falling confidence in the ability of the industry to deliver both profits and social value.

But why did the stock price plummet when SKS did nothing wrong? It had been careful to build trust. It had even nurtured it, building it on top of the community trust systems already in place. Yet, the endeavor still had reached the brink of falling apart.

To be sure, many reasons exist for the crisis. Overall, though, SKS underestimated the fragility of trust. The factors that built that trust up had started to break down, obscured by giddy rates of growth before the crisis.

Even as SKS focused on building trust in itself, the organization neglected other areas that were critical to a strong societal trust in the industry as a whole. The so-called "public goods" needed to adequately govern or police the growth of SKS and the industry overall did not mature nearly fast enough.

Could organized microfinance have done more to forestall corrupt behavior on the part of malfeasants? For example, in India in 2010, there wasn't a well-functioning credit registry. One existed on paper but suffered from lack of enforcement and low participation from MFIs.

This meant that it was very difficult for loan officers to check on the level of indebtedness of recipients before issuing a loan. Some borrowers took loans from several MFIs at the same time, repeatedly paying off one MFI with a loan from another, perhaps sinking into debt, in worst-case situations. Having good data on the aggregate loan exposure of a potential customer, through a functioning credit registry, is a precondition for dealing with this.

The industry association had called for the registry to be maintained. Indeed, SKS had contributed to it, but many others had not, so the registry failed to adequately reinforce this industry norm. One might say that the regulator should have enforced it, but the regulatory muscle is often underdeveloped in emerging markets.

The lesson from this error is that it is incumbent on the industry's entrepreneurs to solve such problems proactively. Throughout the developing world, firms themselves have more responsibility to build these kinds of institutions in the vacuum left by frequently dysfunctional governance.

Having learned the hard way, today SKS voluntarily uses the highest global credit-checking standards. "We have put in place a ton of safeguards and have done far more than anyone in the industry," despite the cost, says M. R. Rao.

"It's the burden of leadership," adds Dilli Raj. "We were the leaders before the crisis. Being the leader, we thought we had to take the initiative, to earn back the trust."

SKS kept its interest rates low to help regain trust, as well. Today, its interest rates are around 19.5 percent, *the lowest in the world* among microfinance firms. Here, SKS is investing in trust, aggressively "returning" money to its customers through ever-lower interest rates.

In the years since the crisis, SKS has climbed back to amassing over $2 billion in market capitalization. Its loan portfolio has rebounded, a sign of the revitalized trust placed in microfinance by large swaths of India's rural citizens. It is investing aggressively in so-called last-mile payment technologies. Its new possibilities were the fruit of a long, patient effort to reassure banks, regulators, and customers, and also to put in place even more safeguards.

All the evidence tells us that trust must be nurtured slowly, and that it can be lost at the first misstep. It took five years for SKS to earn some of its accumulated trust back—from the market, from watchers of the industry, and from borrowers on the ground. Once trust starts to unravel, it can spiral out of control in a headlong, runaway manner.

Reflections

In the outskirts of Mexico City and Hyderabad, two entrepreneurial groups, at Compartamos and SKS, built impressive, financially viable, trust-based organizations to serve the poor atop preexisting social structures. Their histories, through engagement with the capital markets and with the local political apparatus, suggest also that these trust-based organizations, however seemingly robust, must always guard against internal and external attempts to destabilize them, whether inadvertent or conscious.

Even so, these organizations provide stability to the small-scale entrepreneurs whom they help. Indeed, we tend to glorify dramatic change created by entrepreneurs. Such change can be fantastic, yet it still inevitably comes with a great deal of tumult. Some societies lack the mechanisms to allow their populations to stomach this turmoil. Seemingly paradoxically, a degree of stability is needed to foster change. The MFIs described here had to work to create the stability necessary to pursue their goals. They did so by building atop preexisting social norms, thus bringing opportunity at scale to the millions who needed it.

Four

Working as a Team
with the State

The developing world is characterized by widespread mistrust of the state, with government seen as incompetent at best and corrupt at worst. Yet pillorying the state is pointless. In Brazil, the state made a successful push with conditional cash transfers to move people from poverty to subsistence. But would-be entrepreneurs there have stagnated, lacking a bridge to society's mainstream. If one thinks of the different parts of society as members of a team, the situation is much like the selecão—Brazil's fabled football team—which has fallen apart lately. In India, by contrast, an unlikely entrepreneurial partnership between technologists and the state has leapfrogged the world's tech leaders to provide a billion-plus residents a unique biometric identity where none existed earlier. Both Brazil and India spotlight the need to understand entrepreneurship as a team sport for it to have impact at scale.

Societal Teamwork

It was the championship match of the 2014 FIFA World Cup, and the Maracanã Stadium was charged with a muffled enthusiasm.[1]

Enthusiasm, because *futebol* is Brazil's national religion and because the final match was being played in the high temple of *futebol*—in the heart of Rio de Janeiro. And muffled, because it was the Germans and Argentines who were playing for the Cup— *not* the *seleção*, Brazil's storied national team.

The raucous chants echoed around the stadium. They rose and then died out quickly, perhaps as their initiators recalled the still-fresh wound: Germany's 7–1 rout of the *seleção* just five days earlier in the semifinal, the worst loss in Brazil's history.

The Brazilian national *futebol* team jersey features five stars on the chest, one for each of its FIFA World Cup titles—more than any other country. Its players, from Pele to Socrates to Ronaldo, have been larger-than-life figures in society, more powerful in their way than most politicians. In a place where politicians have recently been plagued with corruption scandals, the *seleção* is one of the few national institutions in which Brazilians take much pride. They were widely expected to acquire a sixth star in this World Cup. But by the time they reached the semifinal, Brazil had lost both its tough captain, Thiago Silva, due to yellow cards, and its top scorer and one of the best players in the world, Neymar, to a broken vertebra suffered during a quarterfinal match. And it had long since embraced a more defensive, ugly, and utilitarian style of play than *jogo bonito* ("beautiful game"), the style that Brazil made famous in past decades. What's more, the players, most of them with day jobs at various elite football clubs in Europe and Latin America, never seemed to jell as a unit. Brazil's *futebol* fans (the majority of its 200 million citizens) had watched in heartbroken disbelief as the German team trounced the Brazilian team in the semifinal.

Despite this disappointment, the World Cup still represented a victory of sorts for Brazil. Before the tournament, there had been widespread concerns among officials at FIFA (the international *futebol* governing body) and the press that Brazil wouldn't be ready in time. Yet everything had turned out fine. For two weeks, Brazil had smoothly and efficiently hosted the tournament. The buoyant closing ceremony, with bands and samba dancers celebrating across the field, signified an arrival on the world stage for Brazil.

Still, the Brazilians in the crowd used this occasion to vent their displeasure at their absent president, Dilma Rousseff (who later would be impeached due to controversial allegations of mishandling the federal budget).[2] Protests had roiled the country in the year leading up to the Cup. Half a million people had filled the streets of Rio. Accusations of bribes passing between contractors and politicians raged rampant. Romário, one of Brazil's greatest former *futebol* players and a member of Parliament, called the tournament the "biggest theft in history." It was telling that, in this *futebol*-mad country, people were holding up signs outside the stadiums that read: "We don't need the World Cup, we need money for hospitals and education." They wanted "FIFA-standard" spending on these and other basic needs, like transportation infrastructure, food security, and jobs. The protests were a vivid reminder that Brazil was still very much a developing country, with huge income inequality and millions living in slums known as *favelas*—with aspirations, but no obvious way out.

For many Brazilians, "white elephant" stadiums like the Maracanã represented the gap between the society they wanted and the one in which they lived. Indeed, the presence of such stadiums, along with the lack of unity in the performance of the *seleção*, offers a parallel with the story of Brazil's much-vaunted efforts to alleviate poverty. By the time of the World Cup of 2014, Brazil had in fact made significant strides, largely due to a program known as Bolsa Família, halving the number of those living in extreme poverty over the previous decade.[3] But that progress was in danger of stalling, because, just like their *seleção*, Brazilian institutions and entrepreneurs still were not playing a macro-scale *jogo bonito*. They simply were not playing like a team.

Bolsa Família in Brazil

The richest 1 percent of Brazilians have as much household income as the poorest 50 percent combined. Brazil thus has one of the highest levels of income inequality in the world. These data are superficially at odds with the vague narrative of Brazil as a (relatively) harmonious "melting pot." The Brazilian passport is allegedly the most coveted in the world on the black market, since Brazil is so racially and ethnically diverse almost anyone can pass as Brazilian. Today, it is home to the largest number of people of African descent of any country except Nigeria.[4] São Paulo is home to a huge community of people of Japanese extraction: 1.5 million, the largest number outside of Japan.[5] There are 700,000 "Amerindians" in the country, native peoples who live mostly in the Amazon and the northwest interior. In addition to Portuguese, there are sizable numbers of descendants of Italian, German, Spanish, Chinese, Polish, Syrian, and Lebanese immigrants.

But many Brazilians acknowledge that their country still struggles with the dark legacy of a past characterized by pervasive racism and economic exploitation. It was the last country in the Western hemisphere to abolish slavery, in 1888. The old tableaux of inequality were the grand colonial estates, financed by money from the Transatlantic slave trade and created on the backs of oppressed laborers on the sugarcane and coffee plantations that persisted well into the early 20th century.

Nowadays, the chasm between rich and poor is most visible in the jarring juxtaposition of the *asfalto*—the "asphalt" world, as Brazilians call it, where services are reliable and laws are generally enforced—of upper-class Rio or São Paulo and the *favelas*—infor-

The jarring juxtaposition of *favelas* and *asfaltos*.

mal settlements or slums—of those megacities. These are essentially two different countries. They are woven together geographically, though not economically. In terms of opportunity, they remain worlds apart. If the *asfalto* is Avenida Paulista, São Paulo's answer to New York's Fifth Avenue, or the pleasant palm-lined boulevards of Ipanema in Rio—with its well-kept parks, gleaming condos, boutique shops, and street cafes—then the *favela* is a jangle of impoverished settlements, unfinished housing, mazelike streets, bundles of illegal electric wires stretching overhead, and zones where ruthless drug trafficking gangs operate as de facto governments.

These two worlds are located uncomfortably right next to each other, sometimes even sitting on top of one another. A runner jogging along Rio's Copacabana beach would be able to see *favelas* piling up the steep hillsides above, cheek by jowl with some of the priciest real estate in the world. He or she could smell the fresh fish roasted by vendors who feed rich tourists by day and spend their nights in odorous *favelas* like Rocinha or Morro de Alemão.

In preparation for the *futebol* 2014 World Cup, police and paramilitary units fanned out into the *favelas* of Rio, in so-called "pacification campaigns" intended to push out drug lords and gangs, establishing command posts like an occupying army in hostile territory. Wealthy *cariocas*, as Rio residents call themselves, went on with life as usual; for all intents and purposes those slums, viewed from their sleek apartment windows, might have been in the distant Amazon. In Rio, one can toss a stone between a million-dollar condo and a tin-roofed slum dwelling. Yet few bridges connect these two worlds, either real or metaphorical.

One such bridge does exist, however. In a country that loves *futebol*, one could say that Bolsa Família has been the "Neymar" of government policies—its best playmaker, widely celebrated and extremely productive. It directly and indirectly benefits more than a quarter of Brazil's population—over 50 million people—and is the largest "conditional cash transfer" (CCT) program of its kind in the world. It puts money directly into the hands of impoverished Brazilians as long as they meet certain simple requirements. Experts cite Bolsa Família as a major factor in halving the proportion of Brazilians who live in extreme poverty in the decade since its inception in 2003.[6]

The way it works is quite simple: Families whose incomes are under the poverty line receive a small cash payment, averaging about $30 each month, if they comply with a few conditions. If the attendance of a family's children between ages six and fifteen in school falls below 85 percent, or if the mothers don't follow the vaccination calendar and attend pre- and postnatal health checkups both for themselves and for children under age seven, then the benefits are cut off.

The logic behind Bolsa Família is simple. By investing in the health and education of children, the program aims to help break the intergenerational cycle of poverty. And by putting cash direct-ly into the pockets of poor people (mostly women), the program helps these people make ends meet right now, letting *them* decide how to spend the money most productively.

Early on, critics of the program in Brazil worried that giving money to the poor would reduce their incentive to work and en-courage dependency on the state. However, the data suggest that this has not happened; if anything, it has ensured that the poor are brought to a level where they can contribute further to society. Nor is it the case that another fear—that the per-child payment structure would lead to larger families—has materialized. Overall, World Bank researchers have concluded that the program helped reduce income inequality in Brazil by at least 20 percent, and all at the fairly modest cost of just 0.6 percent of GDP. One study found that for every real (the Brazilian currency) invested in Bolsa Família, 1.78 reais were generated for the economy. The program is also well targeted, meaning that very few cases exist where the benefits go to people who do not really need them.

The success of Bolsa Família, along with a similar program in Mexico called *Oportunidades*, has caught the attention of other developing countries. Many delegations have visited Brazil to learn how to copy or adapt the program in their own countries. Similar CCT programs are now operating in more than forty na-tions, testimony to governments' impact.

This story sounds fantastic. The results are truly inspiring. Yet it's not the entire story, for Bolsa Família's effects appear to have hit a ceiling.

. . .

Bolsa Família began when Luiz Inácio Lula da Silva—or simply "Lula," as he is popularly known—became Brazil's president in 2003 and consolidated several predecessor programs to increase efficiency.

Indeed, combatting poverty and inequality had been the central plank in Lula's populist campaign platform in 2002 when he ran as a member of the Workers Party.[7] "If, by the end of my mandate, all Brazilians are able to eat breakfast, lunch, and dinner each day, I will have completed my life's mission," he said in his inaugural speech. "While there remains one Brazilian brother or Brazilian sister going hungry, we have more than enough reason to be covered in shame."[8]

This was the language of solidarity—what one might expect from a lifelong union leader and populist politician. But it also spoke to the real and deep fissures running through Brazilian society. Lula appealed directly to his fellow Brazilians to consider the fight against poverty in their country as a "team effort." Lula is a rabid *futebol* fan—one of his first acts as president was installing a *futebol* field on the front lawn of the presidential residence. Yet the national mood changed dramatically in just a few years toward the end of Lula's term in 2011 and the beginning of that of Dilma Rousseff, his chosen heir.[9] Lula had largely presided over strong economic growth, but under Rousseff, the economy was slowing.[10]

Tensions arising from inequality remained ever-present, even with the success of a program such as Bolsa Família. The hundreds of thousands of protestors in Rio's streets one year before the World Cup had not been people from the *favelas*. Rather, they were mostly recent entrants to the middle class. This strained class relationship was captured in a hit song, "Middle Class," that ruled the radio waves in 2006 at the end of Lula's first term. The song's singer excoriated the proclivity of some in society to materialism amid others' privation:

Porque eu não "to nem ai"
Se o traficante é quem manda na favela
. . .Toda tragédia só me importa quando bate em minha portat
Porque é mais fácil condenar quem já cumpre pena de vida

Because I don't care
If drug dealers rule the favelas
. . .Tragedies are only real if they knock on my door
Because it's easier to condemn someone who's already serving a life sentence.

The song's success was a pointed reminder that, even though residents of Rocinha and Copacabana alike root for the national *futebol* team, outside of soccer not much else is a team sport in Brazil—and everyone knows it. When some protestors during the 2013 agitation started saying that even military rule (such as that of the 1960s and 1970s) would be better than Rouseff, Rio's State Federation of Favela Associations published an image that soon went viral online. It was a photo of soldiers in helmets driving armored cars down a *favela* street, overlaid with the acerbic message: "Hey, reactionary! Come and live in a *favela*. Here the state is minimal, and there's military intervention."

Those trying to understand Brazil's economic story over the past decade or so—as well as the larger global trends of poverty and development beyond Brazil, from sub-Saharan Africa to South Asia—toggle between the bleak view of the popular "Middle Class" song and the more hope-filled narrative suggested by Bolsa Família's impact.

On the one hand, thanks to a variety of factors, including currency and other economic reforms, Brazil has added 30 million people to the "middle class" in the past decade and has cut in half the fraction of those living in extreme poverty. This is a smaller version of the complicated miracle in China that lifted 500 million out of poverty over the last thirty years, but is nonetheless highly laudable.

On the other hand, millions of Brazilians still haven't benefitted from that growth. This gap generates costly social strife, lost opportunities for millions, even violence at times. For those at the bottom, a government hand up the socioeconomic ladder, with its checks and balances, is both necessary and feasible.

Even those who benefited from Bolsa Família might have reached the limits of their climb up this metaphorical ladder. While someone in poverty might be lifted to a less precarious economic existence through these programs, is it possible that these could also provide enough of a bridge from the *favelas* to the *asfalto*? If not, then an opportunity exists for entrepreneurs to step up and fill this void. With people working together and establishing a trusting relationship between all parties—the poor, the rich, the government, and aspiring entrepreneurs among them—change may be possible at an even larger scale than has been achieved.

Or is Bolsa Família mostly a story of limits, of fast progress and then hitting walls, like a *futebol* team that has relied too much on one player, fallen apart, and stopped playing like a trusting team?

To understand the answers to all these questions, one must view Bolsa Família on the ground.

A Bolsa Família Story

Standing in the middle of his small snack shop, Antonio folds his arms and admires the cases of sweet and savory treats he sells to hungry members of his community.[11] "I am always thinking about how I can make things beautiful and inviting," he says. He gestures toward a gleaming, rotating display of small sweets. "That's our latest investment."

The shop is located on a busy street in the surroundings of Campinas, a metropolis in the state of São Paulo, one of the world's most populous urban areas. Antonio and his wife Joana, a couple in their mid forties, run it together. Their oldest child, a university student, does the finances. The youngest child helps make the small cakes and pastries, of which they sell thousands each week.

Drug dealers and addicts loiter outside on the curb as loud traffic surges past a line of broken-down cars. The shop, a modest but clean and cheerful space, seems like an island of care in a sea of neglect and despair. When asked about his monthly revenue, Antonio says it is 20,000 reais per month. But after several customers get up from one of the two plastic tables and leave, he adds, "Actually it's 100,000 per month." He doesn't want to broadcast that fact to the *favela*. Since the advent in 2014 of Operation Car Wash (*Lavo Jato*)—a euphemism for the ongoing and systemic anti-corruption proceedings riling the country—and the subsequent impeachment in 2016 of President Dilma Rousseff for "creative accounting" (*pedeladas fiscais*), Antonio has grown skeptical of Brazilian institutions. Antonio therefore doesn't trust the banks and instead invests most of his cash in equipment for his business: the freezer, the dough-roller, the mixer, the Italian ice-cream maker, the jukebox, and the rotating sweets display.

Antonio stopped going to school when he was twelve years old. "But I see the world with a broad lens," he remarks. In his street philosopher's manner of speaking, he talks a lot about choices. Look at those drug dealers and addicts, he warns his kids: "You could go that way, the way of drugs, and get stuck here. Or you could go *our* way. It's slow, but we'll get out of here eventually."

Antonio worked for many years loading and then driving trucks. His rounds sometimes took him deep into the city's affluent *chique asfalto* areas. "When I was a driver," Antonio says, "I'd see kids on the streets getting *trotes* once they were accepted at the universities." *Trotes* is an initiation ritual of sorts for newly admitted college freshmen. Older students paint their youthful faces and send them out to beg for money on the streets, to pay for a barbecue party for the upperclassmen. "I saw them having fun, and I'd think, 'With this salary, and several kids—one with a severe health issue—I will never get there.'" Antonio meant that he would never be able to send his own kids to college. They would never be out on those streets, faces painted in that joyous ritual, celebrating their arrival at the university, bridge to a land of opportunity.

Today, Antonio has a child attending one of those universities. Two others are well on their way to their own *trotes*. Another— the one with the health issue—is in stable condition, thanks to the health insurance Antonio purchased for the whole family.

Bolsa Família created the conditions for Antonio and Joana, to create these positive results for themselves.

Joana's parents were rural unskilled laborers. When her father passed away, shortly after she finished fifth grade, Joana dropped out of school in order to live with her older sister and seek work. "My mother worked her whole life to raise us; she never gave up on us," she recalls. "I started helping her when I was six years old, and for many years I worked in tedious dead-end jobs."

Antonio and Joana met soon after she moved to the city. Antonio was a *"boia-fria"* – slang for itinerant farm laborer — from the impoverished northeast. The *boia-fria* have traditionally been on the lowest rung of Brazil's economic ladder. As rural migrants, they would go wherever plantations needed their labor. The name comes from *buoy*, slang for "meal," and *fria*, which means "cold," as these men would bring their cooked lunches with them in un-insulated containers, so their food would always get cold by lunch-time. Bosses piled them onto trucks and ferried them to the fields, their work varying with the seasons. Antonio was one of legions of *boia-fria*. More than 30 million Brazilians left the countryside in the 1970s, swelling its *favelas* in their search for a better life.

Within three months of meeting, these two young rural strivers were a couple, barely out of their teens. Joana's sister soon fled illegally to the United States in search of better prospects. "I decided to move in with Antonio," Joana says. "We put our toothbrushes together. We were both honest, hard-working people. Antonio treated my son from a previous relationship as his own."

For years, Antonio battled the city's hellish traffic and pollution on his delivery routes. Joana cleaned the homes and hotel rooms of the wealthy. They combined their incomes, scrimped, and saved, just like millions of poor parents in developing countries around the world.

But they had to be creative to get beyond a hand-to-mouth existence. So Antonio bought a tiny patch of land and built a small shop, paid for by the sale of a car he had long saved for and bought.

"This place was a hole!" he says, sweeping his arm to take in two modest but tidy double-storied concrete buildings. Housing is so expensive in the city, even in *favelas* like the one the couple ended up in, that he decided to basically *make* his own building lot, and then turn those high rents to his advantage. "I brought in soil, gathered friends, built the building—and then revenue started coming in when I began by renting out parking spaces."

Once the couple had their first child together, they qualified for another revenue stream: Bolsa Família. Households are eligible for Bolsa Família benefits if they have children and their per capita monthly income is between 60 and 120 reais; or if their income is between 0 and 60 reais per month, regardless of whether they have children. So, at that time Antonio and Joana received 80 reais a month, and when their oldest child started school, a total of 160 reais. It was roughly one tenth of their income—a significant boost, since only Antonio was working at the time. Joana took care of the young kids and did *"bicos,"** he says—small jobs from time to time, "like a bird dipping its beak here and there."

"Bolsa Família came in and helped us buy milk, medication, shoes for the kids," Joana says.

"I wouldn't let anyone touch it; we saved it for the kids," Antonio agrees. "We really depended on it when we lived in the alley, ten years ago."

Thanks to the combined income from Bolsa Família, renting the garage, and their work, they were eventually able to construct a small house on top of the shop space—the comfortable rooms where they now live.

"Yes, fundamentally, Bolsa Família helped us get started," Antonio says. "It covered the basics. Eventually, if I didn't have Bolsa Família, we would have made it, but only many years later. So it accelerated our timing to own a business."

Bolsa Família, in short, began to *create the conditions to create* for the young family.

Success can sprout from the unlikeliest places. Antonio's had its start in an unfortunate turn of events. Without their knowledge, and to their consternation, one of their teenaged children, Marcelo, had illegally gone to work with cousins in the United States. After a few months, Marcelo became ill and, after seeking medical care, was deported. Upon return, the only income Marcelo could generate was by making snacks he learned how to prepare in the U.S.

Joana and Antonio saw an opportunity to help their family and themselves. They had already been selling small pastries and coffee to neighbors out of their little shop. Now they saw potential for bigger things, if only they could improve the quality and selec-

---

* Spelling in Portuguese; pronounced like "beacos."

tion of their snack items. About six years ago, they decided to put all their energy into this venture. From this serendipitous start, they nursed a young business to support the whole family.

In their first week, Antonio was surprised to realize that they had made 1,000 reais, almost as much as they had been making in an entire month. Once they tasted this small success, they wanted more, but soon realized it would require embracing some risk. Antonio talked to equipment manufacturers who agreed to let him pay for a pastry fryer in installments. Later, a cousin, impressed by Antonio's success, helped pay it off. They thought ice cream would be a big seller, too, so they found an Italian ice-cream machine on MercadoLivre, the "eBay" of Brazil where one can buy practically anything through a smartphone.

Antonio and Joana seem to balance each other. Joana kept pushing them to take smart risks, to expand what was possible. They have proven to be ideal teammates in business, just as in their twenty-five years together. Their combined ideas and complementary temperaments created an atmosphere of psychological stability. And the Bolsa Família income stream reinforced their financial stability. These, in turn, permitted risks and investment.

"She encouraged me," Antonio says. "And the machine paid for itself quickly." Within the first three weeks of using the ice-cream maker, they had made 3,000 reais. With that, they "graduated" from Bolsa Família. "We depended a lot on Bolsa Família," Antonio recalls. Once they were on a sound footing, they decided to forgo the benefit. "We visited the local Caixa Economica [state-sponsored bank] and resigned from the program. It was time to give this benefit to someone else."

One day, he says, he went to look at a car. It would make their lives easier and be useful for the business, but it cost 78,000 reais. Too much, he thought. But Joana said, "You want the car, you can afford it, go and buy it."

So he put the cash in a kid's backpack and went back to the lot. The salesperson had been dismissive and hostile before, assuming Antonio didn't have the money. When he returned, Antonio insisted on seeing the manager. "I didn't want that first salesman to get the commission," Antonio says with a laugh. He unzipped the kid's backpack with the 78,000 reais in it, and the manager started treating him with respect.

Now they have a car and five employees, including two deliverymen, and they seem to have momentum. The shop has food service equipment worth more than 250,000 reais. They sell more and more outside their immediate neighborhood, reaching new customers via their busy social media pages.[12] Antonio dreams of expanding to other locations.

"Imagine other units in the city center. Every day I get more excited!" he says. It doesn't seem so far-fetched, since they've already delivered their delicious *coxinhas*—shredded chicken fried in dough—to downtown addresses.

The family credits Bolsa Família with providing both a catalyst and a safety net for their risk-taking. "Bolsa Família was the trigger—when I needed it, I had it, but I didn't coast on the benefit," Antonio claims. They know many people who received the cash transfer but did not invest it wisely, and failed to "revolutionize their work."

With this precious boost, Antonio insists, "You must do something to improve your lives!"

His goals all along were the education of the kids, a dream that now seems secure, and taking care of his wife, his teammate. On the latter front, they reached an important milestone several years ago. Antonio finally took Joana out on a dinner date. "In twenty-five years it was our first restaurant," he says.

When they sat down, they were no longer invisible, no longer daytime travelers into the *asfalto* world. They had earned their seat at that table. They, once the servers of this wealthy part of town, were now themselves being served. It was a proud moment.

Today he has another new goal: "I want to employ many people." He dreams of opening several new branches of his shop so that he can do so. Indeed, both Joana and Antonio talk of wanting a better clientele than the drug dealers who come in—but how to leave the *favela*? Should they try to reach the *asfalto*? Would they even be happy? Would they feel a sense of belonging once they got there?

The *favela* has its bitterness and challenges, yes, but it also has a tight sense of community. The drug dealers don't mess with him and his family, Antonio explains, because they respect each other. "I'm safer here than I would be downtown, because they know me here."

It's still a difficult life. Antonio and Joana get up early and work hard, in a place that's full of violence and addiction. But the couple and their children seem to have found a foothold in Brazil's middle class. Still, they face more hard work to further build their business. They would have to formalize and legalize their accounts, instead of keeping the typical *favela* loose handshake arrangements they have with suppliers now.

And they would have to outgrow the suspicion revealed by a brief story Antonio tells. Several years ago, they thought about taking out a loan to finance the construction of their small house above the shop. Antonio told Joana to get dressed up in her finest clothes, and they went to the bank. The manager seemed skeptical at first.

"Do you have a restaurant license?" he asked sternly.

Antonio's first thought was, *How do we get out of here?* But the manager softened when he learned about their monthly revenue. He offered them coffee and started explaining the interest rates on their loans. Antonio had dropped out of school young, but making beverage deliveries made him good at arithmetic, he says. Antonio says he knew right away that he could never pay that rate by driving a truck. "With the interest, a 10,000 reais loan would mean that in one year's time I would owe 22,000. It would never work."

They told the manager that they needed time to think about it. They left the bank and never went back, resolving to keep their money under the mattress. "Let's just work harder," he told Joana.

That philosophy, and the small but steady early boost from Bolsa Família, has taken them far. Yet to expand their business further—to employ hundreds, to have a place in the city center—they would have to get beyond their skepticism of banks. The family would have to take on and manage debt, deal with health inspectors and grantors of all sorts of business licenses, navigate bureaucracies. They would have to engage with formal, sometimes frustrating, institutions in order to make it in the *asfalto* world. They would need to trust these institutions of the *asfalto* world, and these institutions would need to trust them, as well.

To do all of that, Antonio and Joana needed something that goes well beyond the simple stepping stool of Bolsa Família. Even with all their success, they still need a bridge to reach that world.

Bridges to Society's Mainstream

Alexandra Brentani, a dynamic public health researcher and social worker, is working on just such a new "bridge" between the *asfalto* and the *favela*.[13] A mere ten minutes north from the University of São Paulo, where Alexandra works as a professor of preventative and social pediatrics, lies Favela Vila Nova Jaguaré, one of the oldest informal settlements in the city. First settled in the early 1960s, it was largely razed in 1994 by city authorities, and then rebuilt, brick by brick, by its residents. Today, about 17,000 people call it home.

At the primary health center in the heart of the *favela*, a line of patients has already gathered outside by 8 a.m. Inside, a dozen mothers with young children sit in a clean, basic, undecorated waiting room. Stacks of paper—each family's medical records—are piled neatly behind a desk.

Alexandra and her colleagues work out of this clinic, training local healthcare workers to conduct home visits in the slum with the goal of improving primary health outcomes for mothers and young children, as part of an outreach program called Projeto Região Oeste (Western Region Project). Families in communities like Nova Jaguaré frequently move around, as they encounter setbacks or new opportunities, so tracking them can be a challenge. Losing track of them can be tragic.

"Child mortality is highest in the first week and first month" after birth, Alexandra explained, "so if we use conventional pediatrician visits after a month, these kids will be dead."

While Bolsa Família has increased the numbers of mothers and children going to health clinics for basic care, as well as the frequency with which they do so, Alexandra's project is trying to improve the quality of the care they receive. The urgency of the need here has led her and her colleagues to experiment with new systems for gathering information, as well as diagnosing and treating medical conditions in the community.

"We're developing tablet- and phone-based solutions to give to primary health workers," she explained. These new apps are designed to help the relatively low-skilled "front-line" health workers become more efficient and effective.

The buildings on either side of the health center—open twelve hours a day, Monday through Friday, providing pediatric, dental, gynecological, and family health services—were painted in cheerful primary colors. But this main building of the health center had metal gates and steel bars and mesh covering the windows. These were reminders of the crime that plagues many *favelas*, often because of violent competition between drug trafficking gangs. Tablets and apps aren't going to be enough to get past these barriers.

"There is less violence in this *favela* than others, because there is only one drug lord," Alexandra said. This man lives in the slum, and, as the sole authority, maintains an informal kind of law and order; and therefore an uneasy peace reigns. He and his colleagues sell drugs unimpeded, and provide basic services like garbage collection and arbitration of disputes, much like an old-world mafia. But thanks to his core business, Alexandra said that drug-related problems were on the rise. More adults were smoking crack, and the psychiatric damage associated with those addictions were spilling over into families and threatening children's health.

Coaching health workers and listening to patients from the community, Alexandra is part doctor, part social worker, and part entrepreneur. She has a warm but crisply efficient matter-of-fact manner, a result of her laserlike focus on improving the health of mothers and children in Nova Jaguaré. If that means she has to deal with unsavory characters such as drug traffickers, then so be it. The plague of drugs and drug-related crime in the *favelas* is a problem with deep structural roots and no easy solution. To save lives here and now, she must work within the constraints that are particular to Nova Jaguaré.

"We have regular meetings with the leaders of the *traficantes*, to let them know what we're doing," she says. "If we don't, they won't let our medical workers into the *favela*." In other words, she has had to build trust with the *traficantes*, beyond just the mothers and the community health workers. Tablets, smartphones, and apps are useful up to a point, but there's no substitute, she has found, for walking through the neighborhood, talking to the residents, and coming back again and again to show that she and her team are in it for the long haul.

To see what that entails, meet Gabriela, an employee of the Projeto. She explains her daily routine. She does eight visits per day, each lasting about twenty minutes. The rest of her eight-hour day is filled with tasks in the central office, where she enters data, undergoes training, and preps the list of homes to visit the next day. Gabriela's only qualifications: She has to be able to read and write, and she must live in the community she serves. She wears jeans, a sweater, and a blue vest that identifies her as a "community health agent," with an ID badge clipped to it. The rest of her equipment is a big shoulder bag, a clipboard, and sturdy black shoes, practical garb for someone who covers many miles each week.

Gabriela embarks on her planned itinerary, climbing the steep, twisting streets of Nova Jaguaré. Alexandra explained that some of these homes sell for between US$5,000 and US$10,000 without a title. Once the city gives a title and everything's legal, the price jumps to $40,000 or $50,000. In 2011, 25 percent of the population in Brazil had an average annual income per capita of about $1,300. Affording a $40,000 home for that population would be out of the question.[14]

On reaching the first address on her itinerary, Gabriela is invited into a clean but modest home to visit with the resident, a mother of three in her early twenties who had migrated from a remote part of Brazil's interior. The woman's sister lives on the floor above, her mother on the floor below. It is a solid, clean, functional house.

With an easy smile, her hair pulled back into a practical bun, and a quiet, soothing manner, Gabriela asked the young mother a steady stream of questions. She wrote down the answers by hand on her clipboard, even though she had the tablet/smartphone the Projeto had given her.

"I don't like to type into the phone when talking to a client," Gabriela says. "It makes them feel ignored." So she types the information into the tablet later in the day. The questions themselves track both the quotidian and the major events of a life: changes in residence, health, pregnancy, deaths. There are questions about plants in the household, and whether there is stagnant water inside or out, since mosquito-borne dengue fever is a big problem in this *favela*. In her big shoulder bag are the notebooks she uses to track medical information for each child. The mother is supposed to fill it out, but she hasn't kept up with it. She gives the young mother a gentle lecture about its importance. "You write down the height here, and the weight here, and any illnesses here."

Soon she is back on the street, on her way to the next house. Alexandra, who has come along for the visit, is offering some positive feedback on the exchange when Gabriela runs into a neighbor. The two women exchange greetings with an easy familiarity, as though picking up a conversation recently left off.

"*Oy, tudo bom?*"

"*Sem, tudo bem.*"

"*Como vão as crianças?*" ("How are the children?")

They chat for a while in this vein, discussing the health of the woman's family. The agent lets her know she would be coming by her house within a few days, as part of her rounds. Gabriela reminds her to take her blood pressure medication, and, if an issue comes up sooner, she can go to the clinic. They say goodbye and Gabriela walks on.

. . .

These encounters in Nova Jaguaré's maze of streets demonstrates the web of trust being woven in this tight-knit community. Moreover, the Projeto represents the new tendrils growing between the worlds of the *favela*, the *asfalto*, and beyond. For example, the Projeto connected the *favela* to the world of the university just a mile away, with its abundant resources and competent, compassionate problem solvers like Alexandra. The health clinics throughout the Região Oueste stayed in regular communication with academic institutes at the University of São Paulo, which offered training, monitoring, financial, and practical support. And the institutes, in turn, were collaborating with colleagues at Harvard.

The project is young and the results are far from in. But it is precisely these kinds of trust-building, innovation-driven efforts that need to be launched, replicated, and scaled up if Brazil's millions of Bolsa Família recipients and *favela* dwellers and *boia-fria* are to get "unstuck"—and to reach the middle class.

Alexandra's connection to premier universities and education in the *asfalto* signals her role as a bridge builder. Not only is her entrepreneurial endeavor providing a bridge between *favela* and *asfalto*, her research works in this way, as well. Her data and analysis get published in health-related publications, bringing down barriers in the *asfalto* caused by unfamiliarity with the true problems in the *favelas*.

A Powerful Combination of Private Entrepreneurship and State Action in India

Money is important, but it might not always be sufficient to enable upward movement for the poorest in society. Even more foundational is having a simple way to establish and authenticate one's identity. For example, consider its role in Brazil, where a property's sale price in the *favela* increases tremendously when it has been registered with the government and an individual can prove ownership. Antonio and Joana will have to deal with licensing for their business in order to move to the *asfalto*, another way of signifying that they are trusted folks. Significant benefits exist simply by being in the government system, both to ensure access to government services and to provide others with the trust that they are dealing with individuals whose backgrounds and antecedents they can authenticate. It would be impossible to even administer something like Brazil's Bolsa Família without the institution of a valid government ID.

On the other side of the globe, the experience of the Government of India's Unique Identification Authority of India (called UniqueID) teaches us one way in which government can work with private entrepreneurs, rather than in opposition to them, to provide not merely an identification system but one that has leapfrogged the systems of even the developed world in ambition and reach.[15]

· · ·

When it came time for India to establish UniqueID and work toward introducing an ID system for over a billion people, the government took a bold step. Rather than antagonizing the private sector with its approach, the government welcomed into its inner sanctum a card-carrying member of India's business elite, Nandan Nilekani, who had justifiably achieved fame and celebrity on the world stage by that time. He readily volunteered his services.

"I am but an accidental entrepreneur," Nilekani protests.

His track record belies this, however. A disagreement at his first job of three years, Patni Computer Systems, had led him to cofound a company named Infosys in 1981. From his initial investment of US$250, plus small sums of money from his fellow founders, Infosys became an enormous company with $6.35 billion in revenues by 2011. By the time Nilekani left Infosys to join UniqueID in 2009, the company had become an information technology (IT) and consulting powerhouse, leading the boom of the Indian IT industry throughout the 1990s and early 2000s. By then, Nandan himself had a net worth in the billions of dollars. He intimately knew the power of technology.

Yet technology wasn't enough. Infosys was the poster child of a new economy in India, one that embraced good governance and championed creating value, not only for the founders of the company but also for shareholders and society at large. It had to be seen as trustworthy in order to attract business from established corporations in the West—the clients it sought to serve—because those firms were used to seeing India as a governance backwater in the 1980s and 1990s.[16]

"People called . . . [Infosys] India's 'new economy' company. . . . They still call us that," Nilekani remarks. "For Indian consumers . . . IT has emerged as a tool to sidestep weak systems. People are realizing the 'I' in IT. Attitudes toward technology have undergone a sea change, from the hostility of [the] 1980s and indifference of [the] 1990s to an overwhelming demand for electrification today."

Along with Nilekani, Ram Sewak Sharma was also a major figure at UniqueID—its director general and mission director. He knew firsthand the importance of having a registered, trusted identity with the government. "I come from a small village, Hamirpura, in the Firozabad district of Uttar Pradesh [UP]," he once said. "I asked, as an experiment, 'Who has an identifying document?' Not more than 25 percent had any document. . . . My widowed sister-in-law, who was entitled to Rs 20,000 [US$400] from the Chief Minister's fund because her husband had died, could not cash the check. She had no bank account, since she lacked the documents required by the bank's Know Your Customer [KYC] norms."

Sharma's sister-in-law is, unfortunately, not unique in India. When the UniqueID program began in 2009, most of the poorest in generally poverty-stricken Indian society did not possess identification documents. Moreover, at its launch no unified system truly existed to establish identity countrywide.

The simple problem of not having an identity can have major ramifications for an individual. "Many Indians don't have a school-leaving certificate or birth certificate," Sharma relates. "People are not able to get an LPG [liquefied petroleum gas, used for cooking] connection . . . because they don't have the documents to prove who they are." Most Indians, other than the most destitute, cook with LPG gas, so this subsidy is hugely coveted. In addition to corporate services such as bank accounts, individuals needed myriad documents to claim various government social services—such as pensions, subsidized food, even educational scholarships. In general, these identity-less people are excluded from society. People who needed these services but lacked identification documents had two options: bribe officials for the services or try to manage without the benefits.

The problem was even worse than effectively ignoring the marginalized. Not having a reliable identity system left many millions of people vulnerable to fraud (Indians euphemistically refer to this as "leakage"). Benefits were sometimes claimed by individuals masquerading as those whom they were not. UniqueID "leakage" takes place where nonexistent persons create documents, or where one person creates more than one document, Sharma explains. "Suppose a family is entitled to 5kg of rice on one ration card—if I create two ration cards, I get twice the 5kg. Or if I get two election ID cards, I can vote twice. Or if someone wishes to avoid paying tax, they can open a *benami* account [Hindi for "bank account in a fake name"], using fraudulent documents. . . . So essentially, incentives exist to create multiple or fake identities."

The fraud and corruption was everywhere. This fact not only took away the benefits from the intended recipients of public services, it also created an enormous amount of waste in time, energy, and, of course, money. In 2008, "Below the Poverty Line" (BPL) families paid an estimated $203 million merely to obtain "free" public services. Thus, not only were there errors of exclusion, with deserving people being ignored, but there were also errors of inclusion, with the wrong people receiving benefits. Sharma summed up the situation this way: "I am convinced of the transformational nature of this project—not just for enabling service delivery, but in terms of its inclusion potential."

The Government of India project about which he speaks is the creation of Aadhaar, a unique twelve-digit identification number to grant people a source of identity proof and also to serve as a way to include more people in society. Aadhaar is the Hindi word for "foundation." The UniqueID, the organization behind the Aadhaar, was established on January 28, 2009, as a means of accomplishing this goal.

. . .

Then, the UniqueID was forced to confront the ultimate question: How would it go about registering individuals' identity in a way that can easily be retrieved by them, whatever their class or situation? UniqueID began by establishing a system to match the randomly assigned Aadhaar to biometric data—a photograph, 10 fingerprints, iris scans, and general information such as name, address, date of birth, and gender. The enrollment equipment had to be easy to use and mobile in order to gather information from as many people as possible.

Outfitted with only a few items—a briefcase packed with a laptop complete with enrollment software, fingerprint reader, and iris scanner, plus a webcam, a laser printer, and a monitor—the enrollment officers ventured into the field. To avoid the need to set up brand-new infrastructure and slow the enrollment process down, UniqueID partnered with other public organizations that already interacted with many people to deliver the enrollment services, dubbing these entities "registrars."

Once people arrived at the registrars to enroll for their Aadhaar, they had to confirm their date of birth and their address (those unable to state their date of birth could choose a date, which was then considered final). As one officer described the process, "Enrollment occurs in two languages—English and the regional language. As transliteration occurs simultaneously, the enrollee can check data accuracy." After this initial registration, the recipient was given an Enrollment ID (EID) to use until their Aadhaar was finalized and granted.

Anjali Raina, executive director of the HBS India Research Center in Mumbai, described the process of getting her own Aadhaar: "I was one of the first people to get an Aadhaar card. I actually got one in Bangalore at a camp. . . . I signed up for the card, as I was sure that it would eventually become the de facto identity for all Indians. . . . Getting the card was very easy. There were camps set up all over the country, including at our residential building, at the club, at our office, and so on. The process took about twenty minutes."[17]

Still, people had to be able to trust that the data were secure and that the Aadhaar number could not be duplicated. Once this initial registration process was finished, the person's data went to a high-security data center, where the biometric data were compared to all the previously existing IDs in the system. Users of the system had to trust that neither fake IDs nor multiple identities could be created.

The task to be completed was daunting and enormous. After all, India was hoping to register around 1.3 billion residents overall (around 75 million of whom were homeless)—an unprecedented number globally. By comparison, the U.S. Federal Bureau of Investigation has a database of 66 million criminals plus 25 million civilian fingerprints, and is the next-largest biometric database. The scale and technical complexity of the challenge for India were monumental.

UniqueID enrollment equipment had to be easy to use and mobile.

As a result, the system had to be easy to use. As another enrollment officer stated: "Everyone thought biometric capture required special conditions. We [UniqueID] proved this could be done with minimal conditions of light, in varied temperature conditions and environments—rural, urban, slums, and night shelters. We took some good decisions—that the data would be stored on the computer, not online, and the process would be designed for people with very simple IT skills." The data had to be stored on each registrar's computer, as large swaths of the country often lacked reliable internet access, making a pure online system unreliable. Without extreme simplicity of use, it would have been difficult to scale to a billion-plus people.

Aadhaar was meant to establish trust and include everyone in the system, while at the same time excluding false identities or multiple identities. Aadhaar could also be granted digitally and could provide a platform to which others could digitally interface.

So it was possible to aspire that its widespread use would engender transparency that made corrupt acts increasingly difficult.

. . .

Like the *selecão* in Brazil, UniqueID helped India play as a team. Entrepreneurs and other private-sector talent teamed up with the government to achieve massive impact on the country in a way that was not possible without UniqueID's foundation. As the first employee of UniqueID, Nandan Nilekani had the freedom to build the organization from the ground up, including hiring other entrepreneurs from his technology world as well as entrepreneurially minded individuals from the Indian state.

Ram Sewak Sharma, for example, was a senior official who had been influential in the move to bring more computers into a government whose working processes were sometimes anachronistic. UniqueID worked assiduously to make this new-age government department hospitable to talent from global firms such as Intel, McKinsey, and General Electric, as well as from technology hotspots like Bangalore in India and Silicon Valley in the United States. UniqueID also created opportunities for sabbaticals and internships for people who could only work for a short time before returning to their companies.

Of course, this unlikely combination of technologists and bureaucrats presented its own set of challenges. "This motley mix brought some tension, but also dynamism," Nilekani remarked. As another volunteer put it: "[Nilekani] assembled a star team from different disciplines. . . . For people from the private sector, it was an exercise in understanding how government policy making works." This new combination of government and private-sector experts, both trusting each other, allowed for the exploration of new ideas for dvelopment of a significant government program.

. . .

With this combination of leaders involved in the workings of UniqueID, each design decision of the Aadhaar system was carefully debated and chosen.

For example, signing up for Aadhaar was made voluntary rather than mandatory. One might think making the Aadhaar mandatory would be the best way of reaching scale quickly. But with limited means of enforcing such a large requirement, plus a desire to create a system in which people *wanted* to participate, the team realized that making the Aadhaar "demand-led" would be more sustainable.

"If Aadhaar confers no entitlement, why should anyone sign up for this?" Sharma asked. "If I make it compulsory, I need to create a legal framework, and this will become a barrier to accessing benefits. . . . At first there will be no one with Aadhaar; so if I mandate that the public distribution system will deliver subsidized food and fuel only to those with Aadhaar, I shut out everybody and defeat my purpose."

Nilekani explained, "Demand-led and voluntary is the only sustainable way. Making it mandatory does not mean it will happen. Partner agencies can make their own use of Aadhaar mandatory." In addition, the group of experts setting up Aadhaar kept in mind that its goal was to register as many people as possible in the most inclusive way possible while maintaining trust in the system. This goal was markedly different from that of other nations' systems, many of which were set up primarily to secure national borders. Aadhaar, by contrast, was created to facilitate inclusion into the societal mainstream, especially for those who were most marginalized.

Consequently, while other identification systems might exclude people based on citizenship, UniqueID made sure to include *anyone* living in India for the Aadhaar. For example, for the millions of homeless for whom this would be their first-ever form of identification, even showing the necessary identification materials to join the Aadhaar might prove a challenge. UniqueID made sure that these people could join the identification system as long as they were recommended by a friend, otherwise referred to as an "introducer" (a concept borrowed from India's bank account opening systems). Introducers were protected from getting into trouble for any wrongdoing of the person that they were introducing. The system of trust was among others set up to promote the success of the Aadhaar project.

And once people were enrolled, Aadhaar became precisely what the word meant: a "foundation" of trust on which to build opportunities.

. . .

Within a mere three years, UniqueID had rolled out the new technology and enrolled 190 million people, with the goal of covering 600 million people by 2014. By January 2017, UniqueID had far surpassed that number, having enrolled an astonishing 1.1 billion of India's approximately 1.3 billion residents. Remarkably, in under six years, 98 percent of people in India had been issued an Aadhaar card, and Aadhaar could claim the title of "largest online digital identity platform in the world." Aadhaar had succeeded faster than anyone imagined.

In the years since Aadhaar was created, a number of other government programs and banks began to rely on the identification system to establish trust—another signal that the program is working. For example, the Aadhaar is used when opening a bank account and even when students take important examinations, such as the Secondary School Certificate (SSC) and the Union Public Service Commission (UPSC). Eventually, the ID system could also be used to sign up for a SIM card for a cell phone, to buy a mobile phone, to obtain insurance and retirement plans, to register for property, to file income tax returns, and more. Everyone was building, or was trying to build, on top of the "foundation," whether it was other government organizations or entrepreneurs coming on the scene.

Anjali Raina sums up the situation this way: "The Aadhaar number makes it easier . . . because, earlier, to get a bank account or to get a passport or to even get a mobile number was very painful—you had to produce a lot of documents. Now with just the use of the Aadhaar number you can get all these things done. To that extent it has improved trust in the state."[18]

Microsoft founder Bill Gates praises India's achievement in establishing UniqueID: "Aadhaar . . . is something that had never been done by any government before, not even in a rich country. Now you have something that is going to underlie all of your digital systems, whether it's banking, tax payments, or tracking healthcare records. It is an incredible asset, and it took a lot of bravery and good government leadership to pull that together. In the next several years, India will become the most digitized economy. Not just by size but by percentage as well. All of the pieces are now coming together."

Of course, downsides exist to this type of success, and critics are right to point out issues that need to be resolved. First on the list of concerns is the matter of privacy. What happens if this highly secure system is nonetheless hacked? Second, now that the Aadhaar is largely required for many services in India, both government and otherwise, what happens to the voluntary nature of Aadhaar? This question has become an issue for the country's Supreme Court to take up.

Still, the story remains. Aadhaar demonstrates the opportunity for entrepreneurship from within a government. It shows how individuals can work *with* the state rather than *in opposition* to it. Aadhaar has lived up to its meaning in Hindi—a foundation—by providing anew for others to build atop it.

Reflections

Like Brazil's Bolsa Família, India's program of Aadhaar remains merely a road out of extreme poverty—neither a bridge to the middle class in and of itself nor the answer to all of society's problems. Ultimately, both programs need much more from partners and entrepreneurs to make their effects felt. These remain works in progress.

Bolsa Família provided a basic amount of capital to reassure recipients in Brazil that they could invest in their futures and take some risks. Aadhaar provided something even more basic than capital, a reliable measure of identity throughout India, so that individuals could even be "seen" by society and the state. In other words, being invisible had been a precursor to marginalization, and the Aadhaar worked to bring people back into the mainstream. Without this ID system, it's difficult to imagine that India's disenfranchised would ever be in a position to take a chance on their futures.

Further, both entities—Bolsa Família and Aadhaar—showed how the state itself can be entrepreneurial. In the case of the former, government progressively refined the targeting and assessment of benefits to those who needed them most, to good effect. In the latter, the government reached out to one of its sterling citizens to effect dramatic change: a radical departure from previous norms in a society that has historically seen mutual distrust between the state and private entrepreneurs.

Bolsa Família and Aadhaar alike show how embracing the state is a precursor for creating a massive impact in developing societies. It's not hard to imagine anew what can happen if a given state and the rest of society can learn to play like the *selecão* with their *jogo bonito*!

Trust: A Coda

Bringing It All Together

On busy Chengfu Road in Beijing's Haidian District, throngs of people mill about, pursuing their daily lives. The skies are heavy with Beijing's now-customary gray smog. Bodies jostle with each other, and there are so many people that it's hard to see the sidewalk. Some listen to iPods, others walk hurriedly, while still others stop to consider a change of direction. The bike lanes are close to the bustling highway where cars speed past calm cyclists—oblivious to how perilously close they are to danger. None of the cyclists wear helmets. It feels like the pedestrian's main job is to avoid getting hit by a car as she walks across the street.

These are people in the most frenzied city in the most frenzied country in the world. People pour out of the Wudaokou subway station further down the street. Grabbing their phones, they click on an app, jump on a bicycle, and ride off into the distance.

Under a blue sign on the corner of the sidewalk sits a neatly arrayed group of bicycles, all ready for use. This scene speaks both to Beijing's history and to its future. Historically, bicycles have always been a main source of transportation in Beijing. Yet ten years ago, these bicycles outside subway stations would have been a mess, strewn haphazardly about the ground, some standing, some lying on their sides. Today, they are smarter-looking and pastel-colored and have locks that respond to cellphone apps powered by discrete solar arrays. Numerous new startups provide free bikes and compete aggressively for market share, hoping to make money by selling advertising space on their bicycles or somehow monetizing the data they collect from tens of millions of daily bike rides.[1]

Just as these startup bike companies have preserved the frantic nature of riding a bicycle in China's busy city streets while organizing and modernizing the process, Taobao—Alibaba's consumer-to-consumer effort, bearing a name that translates to "hidden treasure"—has done the same for the traditional Chinese marketplace.[2]

Alibaba is a recent example of successful, large-scale entrepreneurship from a fast-growing developing country that enables us to revisit the lessons arising from several of the stories I've introduced earlier: the myriad ways of establishing trust; the mindset shift to look at interrelated problems holistically; the building of trust atop preexisting social structures and norms; and the need for working with a state to effect change at scale.

· · ·

Meandering through any traditional Chinese market on a given day, consumers are confronted with a plethora of options, people, and purchases. Part of the process of buying something is finding new pathways through the crowds of people and avoiding tripping over garbage on the ground. Everything is busy and everything is for sale. As I walk past the throngs of people, I can see stalls filled with necklaces, trinkets, food, purses, anything—even fried scorpion snacks on a stick, a traditional item neatly offered even just outside a spanking new Starbucks. People are speaking animatedly around me. Through the crowds, I can hear snippets of conversations from other shoppers:

"How much does it cost?"

"Five kuai." (*Kuai* is a local term for the Chinese currency, the yuan.)

"What? That is too expensive!"

"Four kuai."

"I don't know. I think I will search somewhere else. Too expensive!"

The buyer pretends to walk away. As she does so and just as she is about to disappear forever into the crowd of people pushing past, the seller shouts out: *"Wait! Three kuai!"*

The buyer dramatically returns to the store and pauses for effect.

"Hmm . . . Okay! I will buy it."

This bargaining theater is fundamental to any marketplace interaction in many developing countries. In China, the ritual is completely ingrained in buyers and sellers.

Now, imagine this marketplace but *online*. This is what Taobao does.

Just like the bicycles sitting on the street corner on Chengfu Road, Taobao preserves this frenetic activity, yet reincarnates it for the internet. The Taobao website is exceptionally busy in a way that's familiar to someone accustomed to traditional markets. The platform allows consumers to chat with small vendors or with other consumers (in a C2C, or consumer-to-consumer, engagement). A person visiting the website can buy everything from jewelry to furniture to electronics. They can even bargain, and do so safely. Alibaba, the corporation behind this website, has become one of the world's largest companies and has experienced the largest IPO in New York Stock Exchange history.

Who revolutionized this shopping experience, placing it online with technology? It was an English teacher with modest origins from Hangzhou named Jack Ma.

. . .

Before Jack Ma founded Alibaba, his life had been rather unremarkable, even disappointing. He had failed his college entrance exam three times. He couldn't find any jobs. He had even been rejected from a job at KFC (as the legend goes—twenty-four applicants were interviewed, twenty-three of whom were hired: the one rejection was Jack Ma).[3] He finally became an English teacher, an unexciting career move in China. This was *not* the prototype of a young Chinese person destined for material success. Ma was far from being a hotshot from big-city China, nor was he someone credentialed with educational or professional experiences overseas—whom the Chinese call sea-turtles, *hǎiguī*, since they had traveled great distances.

Jack Ma did, however, see the world differently. His exposure to tourists in the picturesque city of Hangzhou, and facility with English—he started the first "English Corner" in Hangzhou's West Lake, a place for people to practice spoken English—probably predisposed him to appreciate different worldviews. Ma realized that the Chinese had zero presence on the internet, long before this fact entered others' consciousness. He coupled this insight with the visceral realization that people would embrace buying on the web as long as consumers could trust that the experience retained the familiar trappings of the Chinese marketplace—complete with the bargaining and discussion that was essential for reassuring consumers that they had made a good buy. In a mindset change similar to that of other entrepreneurs profiled in this book, Jack Ma knew that all these problems were intertwined and that all needed to be addressed simultaneously in order to succeed.

Taobao achieved this outcome through a number of specific decisions, arrived at with great speed through iterative trial, error, and quick correction. For example, the website included a feature called WangWang that allowed for the near-seamless communication between buyer and seller that's essential to the bargaining process in China. Did the supplier have enough products to meet the buyer's needs reliably? Was the item in question of good quality? At the same time, Ma also introduced tools to inspire further trust in the system, such as Alipay and Trustpass. Vitally, Alipay holds the buyer's money in escrow while the purchased item is being sent to the buyer. Only after the buyer receives his purchase can the seller receive her payment, ensuring that consumers trust that they will not be "taken for a ride," as they say. With Trustpass, the seller can pay Alibaba to authenticate its services directly—to visit the supplier, to kick the proverbial tires in its warehouses and factories, and to inspect its facilities—so that the buyer receives additional assurance from a credentialed third party. In this case, the supplier is, quite literally, buying credibility. With the tools of Alipay, WangWang, and Trustpass, Taobao became much easier for the Chinese consumer to accept. These tools, in sum, created a foundation of trust for Taobao.

By using these tools to establish trust and by emphasizing the importance of re-creating the Chinese marketplace online, Taobao was able to build a winning strategy on top of China's preexisting social structures. This approach was key to Taobao's surprising ability to compete head-to-head with the global e-commerce behemoth eBay, which had entered China with a local acquisition in 2003. eBay was dominant in China at the time that Taobao was launched. But eBay did not build on the preexisting social fabric. For example, rather than focusing on the Chinese consumers' penchant for busy, chaotic marketplaces, eBay instead insisted on the same spare look and feel that the company used in the West and remained blissfully oblivious to Asian bargaining traditions. Indeed, eBay made little effort to invest in the tools to inspire trust in the Chinese market. Trust, born out of familiarity, thus allowed Taobao to best eBay.

. . .

It would seem that up until the point of Taobao's initial success, Jack Ma made solid strategic choices as an entrepreneur in a rapidly transitioning developing country. Still, how did he work with the Chinese state?

At Alibaba's inception, Jack Ma went to the Chinese government. The internet was new at the time. As Ma tells the story, the government was less concerned with helping an e-commerce platform than it was with understanding what to make of this new internet technology—and perhaps how to control it. Jack Ma went his own way when he realized that it was premature to ask for a hand from an uncomprehending state.[4]

Yet as time passed, Ma's emphasis on creating trust with the local Chinese customer worked. The throngs of people in traditional Chinese marketplaces soon could be found on the Taobao website. Taobao began to transform the way that people in China did business. So-called "Taobao Villages" began to emerge literally overnight in China some years ago—starting in Jiangsu, Zhejiang, and Hebei provinces—where entire communities of local residents launched small-scale business operations with virtual storefronts on Taobao. People could buy and sell just about anything on Taobao. Rural and urban Chinese were connected electronically. Rural communities that might have relied on aid no longer needed to. At the time of writing, Alibaba and the other two of the so-called BAT trio of firms—Baidu (an online search site similar to Google) and Tencent (a social networking site and digital media company)—are China's impressive contributions to

the frontier of tech. They were all created by homegrown entrepreneurs. It seems fair, then, to assume that the state has swung
from benign indifference to more active support of its indigenous
entrepreneurs and has made entry by incumbent enterprises from
the West progressively more difficult. Indeed, the likes of eBay,
Google, and Facebook have struggled mightily to enter China.

Still, the interaction between Alibaba and the state comes with
inevitable ups and downs. A few years ago, the Chinese government took Alibaba to task fairly publicly for allegedly not doing
enough to police the selling of counterfeit products on its plat-
forms. The furor seemed to settle down over time, but it was clear
that Alibaba had to maintain its societal license to operate in order
to keep scaling in China. It had to continually develop a modus vi-
vendi of sorts. Part of the challenge of scaling in fast-growing, de-
veloping-country settings—whether it's building on Bolsa Família
in Brazil or on Aadhaar in India or on Alibaba in China—is learning to manage exactly this process.

Reflections

The story of Alibaba and Jack Ma shows all the elements of trust
at play. Ma provided a technology solution. But rather than simply
proffering technology for technology's sake, he ensured that his
business preserved and enhanced customary practices. He built on
the trust already in place in society, understanding that this social
fabric can often be an asset. He looked at the problem in a more
holistic way, adopting a mindset that recognized that problems in
developing countries come in interrelated tangles rather than one
at a time. The key, he understood, was to learn how to embrace
this greater challenge and then how to creatively set boundaries
for the entrepreneurial effort in question. Finally, Jack Ma worked
with the government whenever possible to achieve impact at scale.

Ma thus became one of the most famous entrepreneurs in the world, and, more important, inspired entirely new communities of small entrepreneurs. Their web of trust has enriched the lives of millions of ordinary Chinese, not to mention enriching their savvy entrepreneurs.

At the World Economic Forum in Davos in 2015, Jack Ma made this key point: "For e-commerce, the most important thing is trust."[5] Technology, he recognized, is merely a sideshow without trust. To make a difference, and to solve world problems, the entrepreneur cannot wait for someone else to create trust. In fact, the institutions and mechanisms that one might find in a developed setting—be it a developed country or a mature industry—likely will not exist for the entrepreneur in a rapidly developing setting.

In the developing world, where the mechanisms to foster and maintain trust are generically compromised, it becomes the foremost task of the entrepreneur to *create the conditions to create* through weaving a web of trust.

Notes

Introduction: Trust, Entrepreneurship, and the Developing World

1. Adam Smith, *The Wealth of Nations* (Amazon Digital Services, 2014 [1776]).
2. Adam Smith, *The Theory of Moral Sentiments* (Uplifting Publications, 2009 [1759]).
3. Smith, *Wealth of Nations*.
4. Chris Isidore, "The Great Recession," CNN Money, last modified March 25, 2009, accessed September 21, 2017, http://money.cnn.com/2009/03/25/news/economy/depression_comparisons/.
5. Matthew Harrington, "Survey: People's Trust Has Declined in Business, Media, Government, and NGOs," *Harvard Business Review*, January 16, 2017.
6. All information on South Africa in this section comes from personal experience and the following: Sarah Lockwood, interview by the author, August 3, 2017. Quotations from her also come from this interview.
7. Juvenal, *The Sixteen Satires* (London: Penguin, 2004).
8. This section on Craigslist comes from the following sources: Ken Doctor, "Newsonomics: Craig Newmark, Journalism's New Six Million Dollar Man," Nieman Lab, February 16, 2017, accessed September 21, 2017, www.niemanlab.org/2017/02/newsonomics-craig-newmark-journalisms-new-six-million-dollar-man/; Ryan Mac, "Craig Newmark Founded Craigslist to Give Back, Now He's a Billionaire," *Forbes*, May 3, 2017.
9. All information on *Consumer Reports* in this section comes from the following sources: "How We Test," *Consumer Reports*, accessed September 21, 2017, www.consumerreports.org/cro/about-us/whats-behind-the-ratings/testing/index.htm; "About Us," *Consumer Reports*, accessed September 21, 2017, www.consumerreports.org/cro/about-us/index.htm; Richard Perez-Pena, "Success Without Ads," *New York Times*, December 8, 2007; Edward Hudson, "C. E. Warne Dies; Consumer Leader," *New York Times*, May 21, 1987; Mike McClintock, "Home Sense; Fifty Years of Consumer Watchdogging; In 1936 'Consumer

Reports' Began a Colorful Career of Analyzing What America Consumes," *Washington Post*, August 28, 1986; Paul Hiebert, "Consumer Reports in the Age of the Amazon Review," *Atlantic*, April 2017.

10. "BRAC in Business," *Economist*, February 18, 2010.
11. Much ink has been profitably spilled on BRAC, an amazing organization. All references to BRAC in this book come from a case study that the author wrote, as well as from his personal conversations with its founder and chairman, Sir Fazle Abed. The following is the case: Tarun Khanna, "BRAC in 2014," HBS 9-715-414 (Boston: Harvard Business School Publishing, November 19, 2014).
12. Thomas Hobbes, *Leviathan* (New York: Barnes & Noble, 2004 [1651]).
13. Steven Pinker, *The Better Angels of Our Nature: Why Violence Has Declined* (New York: Penguin, 2011).
14. Jeffrey D. Sachs, *The End of Poverty* (New York: Penguin, 2006).
15. William Easterly, *The White Man's Burden* (New York: Penguin, 2006).

One: The Why's and How's of Trust

1. Tania Branigan, "Three Die in Tainted Baby Milk Scandal in China," *Guardian*, September 17, 2008.
2. Background for the Chinese milk scandal can be found in numerous Western media reports during this period—for example, the *Guardian*, *New York Times*, BBC, and others. For example, "China Dairy Products Found Tainted with Melamine," BBC, last modified July 9, 2010, accessed September 26, 2017, www.bbc.com/news/10565838.
3. Jonathan Watts, "Exploding Watermelons Put Spotlight on Chinese Farming Practices," *Guardian*, May 17, 2011.
4. Dan Levin and Crystal Tse, "In China, Stomachs Turn at News of 40-Year-Old Meat Peddled by Traders," *New York Times*, June 24, 2015.
5. Nicola Davison, "Rivers of Blood: The Dead Pigs Rotting in China's Water Supply," *Guardian*, March 29, 2013.
6. Katie Hunt and Zhang Dayu, "Hundreds of Dead Pigs Fished from Shanghai River," CNN, last modified March 11, 2013, accessed September 27, 2017, www.cnn.com/2013/03/11/world/asia/china-pigs-river/index.html.
7. Edward Wong, "Chinese Search for Infant Formula Goes Global," *New York Times*, July 25, 2013.
8. Tania Branigan, "Q&A: China's Contaminated Milk Scandal," *Guardian*, September 23, 2008.
9. Wong, "Chinese Search."
10. Joseph Kahn, "China Quick to Execute Drug Official," *New York Times*, July 11, 2007.
11. Alexa Olesen, "Using New Media, Chinese Try Out Food Activism," *U.S. News & World Report*, June 15, 2012.
12. "Throw Out the Window," accessed September 27, 2017, www.zccw.info/.
13. Keith B. Richburg, "China's Bloggers Are Taking Risks and Pushing for Change, One Click at a Time," *Washington Post*, June 26, 2012.
14. Tarun Khanna, Nancy Hua Dai, and Juan Ma, "Huaxia: Building a U.S.-Style Dairy in China," HBS 9-716-414 (Boston: Harvard Business School Publishing, rev. November 2, 2016).

15. In 2012, Wu Heng issued a notice saying that he was shifting his attention towards a new website designed to assess societal rumors, in what seems to me to be the true spirit of a serial entrepreneur!
16. Information in this section comes from the Huaxia HBS case, Khanna, Hua Dai, and Ma, "Huaxia"; and conversations with Charles Shao in Beijing and in Boston. See also http://en.saikexing.com/, accessed on December 30, 2017.
17. See, for example, Nava Ashraf, Dean Karlan, and Wesley Yin, 2010, "Female Empowerment: Further Evidence from a Commitment Savings Product in the Philippines," *World Development* 38, no. 3 (March 2010): 333–44.
18. Charles Shao, interview by the author.
19. All the information in this section comes from the following: conversations with the author's student Ma Juan, and information from a working paper that reports the technical details of our analyses: Ma Juan, Zhaoning Wang, and Tarun Khanna, "Why Advertising Safety Isn't Safe? Reminder Effect and Consumers' Negative Response to Information about Product Quality," *INSEAD Working Paper No. 2017/08/STR/EMI*, available at SSRN, January 26, 2017, accessed September 27, 2017, https://papers.ssrn.com/sol3/papers.cfm?abstract_id=2906179.
20. Quotes in this section come from a Metro A.G. HBS case: Tarun Khanna and David Lane, "METRO Cash & Carry in China, 2010," HBS 710-448 (Boston: Harvard Business School Publishing, 2010).
21. All information in this section comes from many interviews done at Amul over multiple years, as well as the participation of some of its executives in the author's classes; as well as the following case study: Rohit Deshpande, Tarun Khanna, Namrata Arora, and Tanya Bijlani, "India's Amul: Keeping Up with the Times," HBS 9-516-116 (Boston: Harvard Business School Publishing, rev. June 16, 2017).
22. "Working with Dairy Farmers," Nestlé, accessed September 28, 2017, www.nestle.com/brands/dairy/dairycsv.
23. "Timeline of the Riots in Modi's Gujarat," *New York Times*, August 19, 2015.
24. The information in this section comes from Verghese Kurien, *I Too Had a Dream* (New Delhi: Roli Books, 2014).

Two: The Mindset Change

1. Specific information on Narayana Hrudayalaya Heart Hospital comes from the two following Harvard Business School cases, the two following videos, and fourteen years of the author's association with Dr. Devi Shetty. It also derives from interviews with Laxmi Mani and others associated with the hospital. HBS cases: Tarun Khanna, Kasturi Rangan, and Merlina Manocaran, "Narayana Hrudayalaya Heart Hospital: Cardiac Care for the Poor," HBS N9-505-078 (Boston: Harvard Business School Publishing, June 22, 2005); Tarun Khanna and Budhaditya Gupta, "Health City Cayman Islands," HBS 9-714-510 (Boston: Harvard Business School Publishing, rev. March 16, 2016); videos: *Narayana Heart Hospital—Part I Pre-Class*, prepared by Tarun Khanna; *Product #: 712802-VID-ENG.Narayana Heart Hospital—Part II in Class*, prepared by Tarun Khanna; *Product #: 712802-VID-ENG.*

2. "And the Winners Were …," *Economist*, December 3, 2011.

3. All information on task shifting comes from the following: Budhaditya Gupta, Robert S. Huckman, and Tarun Khanna, "Task Shifting in Surgery: Lessons from an Indian Heart Hospital," *Healthcare*, September 9, 2015.

4. Egide and Alice are fictional names. This encounter is a composite of conversations with several African patients whom the author met and interacted with at Narayana Health in Bangalore over the years; it was also informed by his visit to Rwanda in 2012.

5. These numbers came from the author's visit to a Partners in Health (PIH) facility in Rwanda in May, 2012. The statements reported here were made on that visit.

6. Josh Kron, "U.N. Report Accuses Rwanda of Massacre in Congo," CNN World, last modified August 27, 2010, accessed September 28, 2017, www.cnn.com/2010/WORLD/africa/08/27/congo.un.genocide/.

7. "Africa's Great Lakes, But Bad Neighbours," BBC News, last modified July 31, 2013, accessed September 28, 2017, www.bbc.com/news/world-africa-23502803.

Three: Building on Existing Social Norms

1. "Compartamos Banco," ACCION, last modified 2015, accessed September 28, 2017, www.accion.org/our-impact/compartamos-banco.

2. "Our Lady of Guadalupe," *Encyclopedia Britannica*, accessed September 29, 2017, www.britannica.com/topic/Our-Lady-of-Guadalupe-patron-saint-of-Mexico.

3. Raul A. Reyes, "Our Lady of Guadalupe Is a Powerful Symbol of Mexican Identity," NBC News, last modified December 12, 2016, accessed September 29, 2017, www.nbcnews.com/news/latino/our-lady-guadalupe-powerful-symbol-mexican-identity-n694216.

4. All information in this section regarding Banco Compartamos comes from the author's field visits to Compartamos sites in February 2009.

5. "Quality Standards," Whole Foods Market, accessed September 29, 2017, www.wholefoodsmarket.com/quality-standards.

6. "Whole Planet Foundation Cookbook," Whole Planet Foundation, accessed September 29, 2017, www.wholeplanetfoundation.org/cookbook/.

7. Philip Sansone and Joy Stoddard, *Liberation Soup and Other Recipes from Microentrepreneurs Around the Globe*, 2nd ed. (Austin, TX: Whole Planet Foundation, 2014).

8. The information in this section comes from the following source: "Whole Planet Foundation," Whole Foods Market, last modified February 27, 2017, accessed September 29, 2017, http://media.wholefoodsmarket.com/news/whole-planet-foundation-launches-2017-prosperity-campaign. The story of Jacqueline was created as a fictionalized example, based on a thorough examination of Whole Foods' public materials.

9. Jake Kendall and Rodger Voorhies, "The Mobile-Finance Revolution," *Foreign Affairs*, March/April 2014.

10. Microfinance sources: Shameran Abed, "5 Reasons Why We Need Financial Services for the Poor," World Economic Forum, last modified September 18, 2015, accessed September 29, 2017, www.weforum.org/agenda/2015/09/5-reasons-why-we-need-financial-services-for-the-poor/; "The 50 Top Microfinance Institutions," *Forbes*, December 20, 2007; "The World Bank Group and

Microfinance," International Finance Corporation (World Bank Group), last modified 2017, accessed September 29, 2017, www.ifc.org/wps/wcm/connect/industry_ext_content/ifc_external_corporate_site/financial+institutions/resources/the+world+bank+group+and+microfinance; Anne Perkins, "A Short History of Microfinance," *Guardian*, June 3, 2008.

11. "The Nobel Peace Prize 2006," NobelPrize.org, last modified 2017, accessed September 29, 2017, www.nobelprize.org/nobel_prizes/peace/laureates/2006/.

12. Madeleine Morris, "Microcredit 'Not the Silver Bullet' for Poverty," BBC Newsnight, last modified January 24, 2011, accessed September 29, 2017, http://news.bbc.co.uk/2/hi/programmes/newsnight/9369880.stm.

13. Michael Chu and Regina Garcia Cuellar, "Banco Compartamos: Life After the IPO," HBS 9-308-094 (Boston: Harvard Business School Publishing, rev. July 18, 2008).

14. The information in this section comes from interviews with Michael Chu in 2015.

15. *The Prize Winner of Defiance, Ohio*, directed by Jane Anderson (Revolution Erie Productions Ltd.; ImageMovers, 2005).

16. "Poor People, Rich Returns," *Economist*, May 15, 2008.

17. Information in this section comes from a combination of interviews with Michael Chu as well as the following article: "Is it Fair to Do Business with the Poor?" World Microfinance Forum Geneva, last modified October 2008, accessed October 1, 2017, www.othercanon.org/uploads/Is%20it%20Fair%20to%20do%20business%20with%20the%20Poor.pdf.

18. "Faculty & Research: Michael Chu," Harvard Business School, accessed September 29, 2017, www.hbs.edu/faculty/Pages/profile.aspx?facId=261321.

19. Information in this section comes from Dean Karlan and Jonathan Zinman, "Long-Run Price Elasticities of Demand for Credit: Evidence from a Countrywide Field Experiment in Mexico," NBER Working Paper 19106 (Cambridge, MA: National Bureau of Economic Research, June 2013, accessed October 1, 2017, www.nber.org/papers/w19106.pdf.

20. Adam Smith, *Wealth of Nations*.

21. The author has been a board member of SKS Microfinance, recently renamed BFIL (Bharat Financial Inclusion Limited), for several years, and this account is based on his recollections and that of the SKS team navigating through this crisis. He also drew from an independent report, *Indian Microfinance: Looking Beyond the AP Act and Its Devastating Impact on the Poor* (Dubai: Legatum Ventures, 2012). Although the organization is now named BFIL, this account will refer to it by the name it had at the time of these events: SKS.

22. Arjun Appadurai, *Culture and Public Action*, ed. Vijayendra Rao and Michael Walton (Stanford, CA: Stanford University Press, 2004).

23. Muhammad Yunus, *Building Social Business: The New Kind of Capitalism That Serves Humanity's Most Pressing Needs* (New York: PublicAffairs, 2010).

24. This information comes from the following: "Discredited," *Economist*, November 4, 2010.

25. Abhijit Banerjee et al., "Help Microfinance, Don't Kill It," *Indian Express*, November 26, 2010.

Four: Working as a Team with the State

1. This account is from personal experience.
2. This action occurred in August 2016 and was reported by many Western news outlets during that time, including the *New York Times.*
3. "How to Reduce Poverty: A New Lesson from Brazil for the World?" World Bank, last modified March 22, 2014, accessed September 29, 2017, www.worldbank. org/en/news/feature/2014/03/22/mundo-sin-pobreza-leccion-brasil-mundo-bolsa-familia.
4. "Black in Brazil: A Question of Identity," BBC, last modified November 3, 2009, accessed September 29, 2017, www.bbc.co.uk/worldservice/news/2009/11/091102_brazil_black_ap.shtml.
5. Ricardo Geromel, "All You Need to Know about São Paulo, Brazil's Largest City," *Forbes,* July 12, 2013.
6. Ibid.
7. "The Meaning of Lula," *Economist,* October 3, 2002.
8. "Three Square Meals a Day," *Economist,* February 20, 2003.
9. "2011 in Person: Dilma Rousseff," *Economist,* November 22, 2010.
10. Kenneth Rapoza, "Brazil Missing Lula as Dilma Economy Disappoints," *Forbes,* November 30, 2012.
11. The Bolsa Família story in this section is a disguised and composite narrative of a common type of situation in the *favelas,* based on interviews done in Brazil by Priscilla Zogbi, director of the HBS Latin America Research Center, Global Initiative.
12. Brazil is Facebook's third-largest market behind India and the U.S.: www.statista. com/statistics/268136/top-15-countries-based-on-number-of-facebook-users/, accessed March 2, 2018.
13. Interviews with Alexandra Brentani, conducted by the author on July 14–15, 2014.
14. Joe Leahy, "2010 Census Shows Brazil's Inequalities Remain," *Financial Times,* November 17, 2011.
15. The content in this section comes primarily from Tarun Khanna and Anjali Raina, "Aadhaar: India's Unique Identification System," HBS 9-712-412 (Boston: Harvard Business School Publishing, rev. September 10, 2012). The official name for UniqueID is UIDAI, simply called "UniqueID" for ease of reading in this book.
16. Tarun Khanna and Krishna G. Palepu, "Globalization and Convergence in Corporate Governance: Evidence from Infosys and the Indian Software Industry," *Journal of International Business Studies* 35, no. 6 (November 2004): 484–507.
17. All quotes from Anjali Raina come from an interview conducted by Carolyn Brown on August 28, 2017.
18. Ibid.

Trust: A Coda

1. Information comes from the author's personal experience and the following article: Akiko Fujita and Jessica Wa'u, "Chinese Smart Bike-Sharing Service Mobike Rides into Singapore," CNBC, last modified March 21, 2017, accessed September 30, 2017, www.cnbc.com/2017/03/21/mobike-chinese-smart-bike-sharing-service-rides-into-singapore.html.

2. Information in this section comes from several sources: an HBS case by Felix Oberholzer-Gee and Julie Wulf, "Alibaba's Taobao (A)," HBS 9-709-456 (Boston: Harvard Business School Publishing, rev. July 30, 2009), as well as numerous classes the author has taught at Harvard and in China; interviews with habitual Taobao users; videos from a MOOC (Massive Open Online Course) the author developed for HarvardX, taught annually since 2016, called "Entrepreneurship in Emerging Economies," www.edx.org/course/entrepreneurship-emerging-economies-harvardx-sw47x.

3. Ali Montag, "Billionaire Alibaba Founder Jack Ma Was Rejected from Every Job He Applied to After College, Even KFC," CNBC, last modified August 10, 2017, accessed September 30, 2017, www.cnbc.com/2017/08/09/lesson-alibabas-jack-ma-learned-after-being-rejected-for-a-job-at-kfc.html.

4. *Vision, Hope, Trust: Jack Ma*, YouTube, 2017, accessed September 30, 2017, www.youtube.com/watch?v=or1K3Ha8bzI.

5. "Jack Ma Wants Alibaba to Serve 2 Billion Consumers," World Economic Forum, last modified January 23, 2015, accessed September 30, 2017, www.weforum.org/press/2015/01/jack-ma-wants-alibaba-to-serve-2-billion-consumers/.

Index

in Brazilian institutions, 125–28, 135, 142, 146–48

Chinese mistrust of food industry, 29–33, 42–46, 60

in e-commerce, 162–68

Huaxia Dairy's cultivation of, 34–41

in Indian ID system, 153–57

and information credibility, 12–14, 15–16, 43–45

in microfinance borrowers, 90–93, 110–11, 122

in microfinance lenders, 97, 104–6, 112–24

Narayana Hospital's cultivation of, 63–87

and personal security concerns, 7–10, 143–44

and Smith's free-market theory, 5–6, 105

and social norms, 89–93, 97, 110–11, 123–24, 162, 165–66, 167

U

UniqueID system (Aadhaar)
  biometric capture, 152–54
  India's need for an ID system, 150–51

official name, 148, 174n15

participation guidelines, 155–56

success of, 156–59

tech entrepreneurs' involvement in, 148–49, 154–55

U.N. Millennium Development Goals, 22

W

Walmart, 15, 65–66, 68–69, 74

Walsh, Conor, 3–4

Walton, Sam, 15

Wen Jiabao, 30–31, 44

Whole Planet Foundation, 93–94

World Bank, 95, 100, 131

World Cup (Brazil, 2014), 125–27, 130

World Economic Forum (Davos), 69, 168

Wu Heng, 31–32, 45, 60, 171n15

Y

Yelp, 14

Yoplait yogurt, 38–39

Yunus, Muhammad, 96, 100–101

Z

Zeiske, Tino, 45

Zimbabwe, 8

About the Author

Tarun Khanna has spent the past twenty-five years as professor at Harvard. He enjoys creativity in problem solving, both as a researcher-educator and as an entrepreneur across the developing world. His travels take him frequently from his home in Boston to Asia—especially China and India—as well as to the Middle East, Africa, and Latin America. All over the world he has the privilege of working with many of his former students. Two of his crazier current projects involve working with museums in Boston and across Asia to get artists to tango with scientists, and advising the Government of India in its launch of thousands of high school "maker spaces" where youth can tinker with solutions to local conundrums. *Trust* is his second book of stories about creative ventures, after *Billions of Entrepreneurs* (2008), a chronicle from a prior decade of his travels in China and India.

Berrett–Koehler
Publishers

Berrett-Koehler is an independent publisher dedicated to an ambitious mission: Connecting people and ideas to create a world that works for all.

We believe that the solutions to the world's problems will come from all of us, working at all levels: in our organizations, in our society, and in our own lives. Our BK Business books help people make their organizations more humane, democratic, diverse, and effective (we don't think there's any contradiction there). Our BK Currents books offer pathways to creating a more just, equitable, and sustainable society. Our BK Life books help people create positive change in their lives and align their personal practices with their aspirations for a better world.

All of our books are designed to bring people seeking positive change together around the ideas that empower them to see and shape the world in a new way.

And we strive to practice what we preach. At the core of our approach is Stewardship, a deep sense of responsibility to administer the company for the benefit of all of our stakeholder groups including authors, customers, employees, investors, service providers, and the communities and environment around us. Everything we do is built around this and our other key values of quality, partnership, inclusion, and sustainability.

This is why we are both a B-Corporation and a California Benefit Corporation—a certification and a for-profit legal status that require us to adhere to the highest standards for corporate, social, and environmental performance.

We are grateful to our readers, authors, and other friends of the company who consider themselves to be part of the BK Community. We hope that you, too, will join us in our mission.

A BK Business Book

We hope you enjoy this BK Business book. BK Business books pioneer new leadership and management practices and socially responsible approaches to business. They are designed to provide you with groundbreaking and practical tools to transform your work and organizations while upholding the triple bottom line of people, planet, and profits. High-five!

To find out more, visit **www.bkconnection.com**.

Berrett–Koehler
Publishers

Connecting people and ideas
to create a world that works for all

Dear Reader,

Thank you for picking up this book and joining our worldwide community of Berrett-Koehler readers. We share ideas that bring positive change into people's lives, organizations, and society.

To welcome you, we'd like to offer you a free e-book. You can pick from among twelve of our bestselling books by entering the promotional code **BKP92E** here: http://www.bkconnection.com/welcome.

When you claim your free e-book, we'll also send you a copy of our e-newsletter, the *BK Communiqué*. Although you're free to unsubscribe, there are many benefits to sticking around. In every issue of our newsletter you'll find

- A free e-book
- Tips from famous authors
- Discounts on spotlight titles
- Hilarious insider publishing news
- A chance to win a prize for answering a riddle

Best of all, our readers tell us, "Your newsletter is the only one I actually read." So claim your gift today, and please stay in touch!

Sincerely,

Charlotte Ashlock
Steward of the BK Website

Questions? Comments? Contact me at bkcommunity@bkpub.com.